chelseafc

Kings of

EUROPE

UEFA
CHAMPIONS
LEAGUE

Kings of
EUROPE

Photography: Darren Walsh, Chelsea FC; PA Photos; Getty Images
Contributors: Paul Mason, Andy Jones, Mark Conlon,
Richard Godden, James Sugrue, David Antill
Production: Adam Oldfield, Alan Jewell
Design: Alison Barkley

Produced by Sport Media, Trinity Mirror North West

Executive Editor: Ken Rogers
Senior Editor: Steve Hanrahan
Senior Production Editor: Paul Dove
Senior Art Editor: Rick Cooke

Published in Great Britain in 2012 by: Trinity Mirror Sport Media,
PO Box 48, Old Hall Street, Liverpool L69 3EB.
Copyright of Chelsea Football Club.

ISBN: 9781908695352

Printed by KINT Ljubljana

CONTENTS

Munich M⊕MENTS
YOU MAY HAVE MISSED

Think you've seen everything from the UEFA Champions League Final? Think again. In all the excitement we reckon you might just have missed a few things that happened on that magical night in Munich. And we don't mean the extra-time for anyone who left...

1. PRE-MATCH: Taking the scenic route

As he begins his ITV commentary, Clive Tyldesley observes that English teams have won the two most dramatic UEFA Champions League finals (Manchester United in 1999, Liverpool in 2005). He remarked: "Chelsea's path to this final has been dramatic. They have taken the scenic route to Munich all right – almost as if it's meant to be."

2. | PRE-MATCH: Jose says hello

As the players line up while the UEFA Champions League anthem is played, Jose Bosingwa – with a big smile on his face – waves to someone in the crowd while everyone else remains impassive. Bosingwa couldn't have looked more relaxed. Was this an insight into the relaxed mood within the Chelsea camp, while Bayern, effectively playing at home, were burdened with expectation and favouritism?

3. | PRE-MATCH: No loose talk

Roberto Di Matteo talks to assistant first-team coach Steve Holland on the bench, with kick-off just 30 seconds away. Both covered their mouths so the words could not be lip-read. Presumably they knew they were on camera, because of the big screens in the stadium. If so, they ensured the details could not be deciphered by the opposition. Every little detail is vital.

7

4. **FIRST HALF: No room for Robben**

During the first real Bayern surge down the right-hand side, Franck Ribery slipped the ball to former Blue Arjen Robben. Ashley Cole, Frank Lampard and Ryan Bertrand were in position to block his path and avert the danger. Chelsea's intention to suffocate the space around the opposition's main threats was immediately obvious.

5. SECOND HALF: The flag stays raised

A Franck Ribery 'goal' is correctly ruled out for offside. As the ball hits the net, the Bayern substitute Rafinha, who was warming up on the touchline with two team-mates, immediately put his arm up in celebration and rushed to the side of the assistant referee. Although Rafinha had plenty to say to the assistant, the flag remained raised.

Thomas Muller, the Bayern goalscorer, is taken off, and replaced by Daniel Van Buyten. After leaving the pitch, he pumps both fists to the 'home' fans. It was quite a celebratory gesture and perhaps a sign that many wearing red felt the job was done. The Bayern bench appeared quite jubilant, rather than tense.

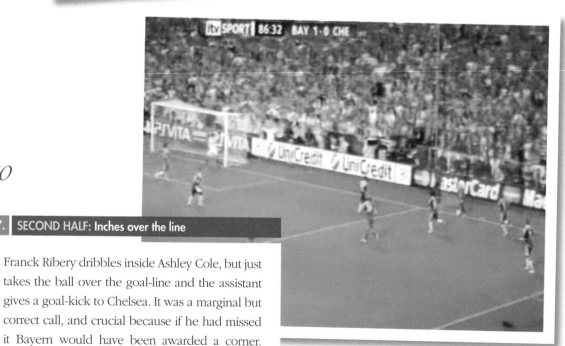

7. **SECOND HALF: Inches over the line**

Franck Ribery dribbles inside Ashley Cole, but just takes the ball over the goal-line and the assistant gives a goal-kick to Chelsea. It was a marginal but correct call, and crucial because if he had missed it Bayern would have been awarded a corner. This was significant because of what followed.

8. SECOND HALF: Time and space

As Petr Cech's goal-kick was headed back into the Chelsea half by a man in red, the ball appears likely to go out for a throw. However, Ribery needlessly jumps into Jose Bosingwa, who is trying to shield the ball, and concedes a free-kick. Chelsea are thus able to re-start play without pressure as the Bayern players retreated to their own half. From the free-kick, the ball is passed from Bosingwa to John Mikel Obi and on to Juan Mata without any of them being challenged. Mata fed Fernando Torres on the right wing, who won a corner. You know what happened next...

9. PENALTY SHOOT-OUT: Andy remains a blue

It wasn't quite on the scale of Gary Neville's hoarse and hysterical yelling as Fernando Torres scored against Barcelona, but former captain Andy Townsend, commentating for ITV, showed his Chelsea allegiances during the decisive moments of the penalty shoot-out. When Ivica Olic's effort was saved by Petr Cech, he could be heard exclaiming, "yes, yes". Bastian Schweinsteiger's failure to convert led to a "oh, come on", while Didier Drogba's winning penalty was greeted with a joyous "yeeesssss".

10. PENALTY SHOOT-OUT: Divine intervention

Didier Drogba is on his knees praying in the centre circle, while Ashley Cole runs back to the centre circle after converting his penalty. During an interview afterwards, Drogba admitted: "I believe a lot in destiny. I pray a lot, as you can see. It was written a long time ago. You have to pray and believe."

11. POST-MATCH: Emotional embrace

As the players celebrated, there was a meaningful embrace between Didier Drogba, John Terry and Frank Lampard – three men who have been through so much together and were pivotal to the club's success in the past eight years. They were the spine of the side and this was the last time they would share such an incredible moment.

While excitement and adrenaline coursed through his body, Drogba, sportingly, made a point of offering words of consolation to his former team-mate Arjen Robben, who was visibly upset.

14

As the players prepare to go up to receive the trophy, Michael Essien jumps on Frank Lampard's back in celebration. Florent Malouda cheekily takes the opportunity to tug at Essien's tracksuit bottoms, briefly exposing the Ghanian's underwear.

14. POST-MATCH: **Parting the blue sea**

When the Chelsea players congregate in the trophy presentation area, Frank Lampard and John Terry are obscured from view as they prepare to receive 'old big ears' from Michel Platini. UEFA general secretary Gianni Infantino desperately tries to get the delirious men in blue to part and allow the moment the trophy is lifted aloft to be seen in full view. Infantino's efforts seem to be in vain but, magically, a gap appears just in time.

Roberto Di Matteo enters the
stadium for the big match

David Luiz is rarely shy of playing up to the cameras, while Juan Mata also arrives (below)

Relaxing at the hotel on
the afternoon of the final

Fernando Torres, Juan Mata and Oriol Romeu
look chilled on the roof terrace of the hotel

A pre-match stretch on the hotel roof

The boss is relaxed
as he looks on

Kalou hopes his new haircut
proves to be a lucky one

Didier Drogba makes sure his muscles
are ready for the rigours ahead

Ryan Bertrand fixes his tie at the
hotel before travelling to the stadium

David Luiz (top picture) and Branislav Ivanovic
look smart in their Dolce & Gabbana suits

The Chelsea team coach is cheered on its way to the stadium by our devoted supporters

I'll take that... Roberto Di Matteo
leaves the stadium with the trophy

Come on boss, we'll help you soak up this historic occasion

The fun and games continue in the hotel pool as the sun comes up on the day after the night before

A European medal in your first season.
Talk about a splash landing for Gary Cahill

Water feeling... Ryan and Didier
share a champion moment

Ryan Bertrand and his medal
are about to get very wet

The team coach was not a
quiet place after the final

John Terry cradles the cup
we had sought for so long

Some empty bottles of
water and a cup full of joy

David Luiz plants a smacker
on the European Cup

There was extra baggage
on the journey home

All together now... Didier and David Luiz
start a sing along on the flight home

Roman Abramovich poses
with the ultimate prize

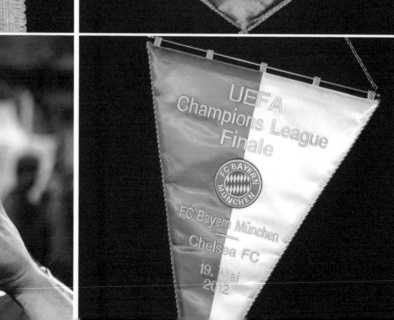

UEFA CHAMPIONS LEAGUE 2011/2012
VALENCIA C.F.
Chelsea FC - Valencia C.F.
6-12-2011

Cupwinner:
1998 - 2000 - 2009
Championship:
1999 - 2002

FC BARCELONA
AL
CHELSEA FC
CHAMPIONS LEAGUE
24-4-2012

MUNICH
FINAL 2012

A European campaign like no other,
the Blues' ROAD TO MUNICH
was the stuff of legend...

UEFA CHAMPIONS LEAGUE 2011/12
FINAL
FC BAYERN MÜNCHEN
vs
CHELSEA FC
MUNICH, 19 MAY 2012

CHELSEA V
BAYER LEVERKUSEN

Stamford Bridge, 14.09.11

Petr Cech:

"Michael [Ballack] was an important player and he was very successful with us. It is always a good memory when you speak about someone who won the Double. He was involved in that team and we won two FA Cups together and plenty of other things, so in the history of Chelsea I think he will be regarded as an important player in the successful years."

Michael Ballack:

"For me personally it is a very big, very important match. I played at Chelsea for four years and it is very nice to be back in London for the first game in the UEFA Champions League. It will be a very emotional moment for me.

When I moved to Chelsea it was a big, big challenge and experience for me at the time to play with so many good players. If I look back I had a very good time. I feel always welcomed by the fans and the club. They treat me always very well and we had success.

It could have been a few titles more. We missed a few chances, but we had some successes and I will remember this always and it is a big part of my career."

41

Chelsea 2
(Luiz 66, Mata 90+2)

Bayer Leverkusen 0

Last minute drama...

David Luiz, with a fine strike midway through the second half, and Juan Mata in stoppage time, gave Chelsea a firm foundation to begin the UEFA Champions League campaign.

This always looked a tough opening game against the side that finished second in Germany the season before and so it proved. Although a Blues side without some of our stalwarts were pretty secure at the back in an opening half in which Daniel Sturridge went closest to opening the scoring, that was not so much the case in the second period and it needed captain-on-the-day Petr Cech to come out on top in a one-v-one with Michael Ballack for the visitors not to take the lead.

Once David Luiz had found the bottom corner of the Bayer net, Chelsea were in the ascendancy.

Best moment...

It would be too easy to say David Luiz's strike, so topping that is the ecstasy of a celebration that showed how pleased the exuberant defender was to be making a difference again after struggling early season with a thigh injury. There was an acknowledgement of the part Fernando Torres played in the goal.

Team news

David Luiz played his first football of the season in place of John Terry and Florent Malouda replaced Frank Lampard on the left of midfield.

John Mikel Obi returned to the holding role with Raul Meireles pushing further forward on the right. Fernando Torres replaced Nicolas Anelka in attack and Petr Cech was captain.

For Leverkusen, Michael Ballack started and received a commemorative plate from Chelsea chairman Bruce Buck before the match for his years of service to the Blues.

First Half

Torres found the ball landing on his foot inside the penalty area with just a minute of the UEFA Champions League season gone. Sturridge was the supplier but the recipient had his back to goal and did well to hook a dropping ball goalwards but just over the bar.

Then came a tale of two disallowed goals, one at each end. First Leverkusen put the ball over the line at the far post but Mikel had been fouled in the build up. Then a move of class from Chelsea saw Mata strike the ball in from wide, Torres flick it on with his foot and Meireles continue the trend of back-heel finishes, but he was rightly flagged offside.

Torres was booked on eight minutes for the type of challenge on Leverkusen centre-back and captain Rolfes that often gets punished in Europe. Moments later the Spaniard was found by compatriot Mata inside the area again but after taking a touch past a defender, the German side's keeper Leno saved the shot with a dipped arm. The 19-year-old between the visitors' posts would perform well throughout the game.

There was almost a goal out of next to nothing when Ivanovic's long punt forward was punched out with two fists straight onto the head of Malouda but from a long way out, the Frenchman's hurried header went wide.

Chances proved harder to find in the middle part of the half as Leverkusen settled.

Ballack's endeavour won a couple of free-kicks in the Chelsea half but there was little threat to Cech.

Then a mistake by Castro gave Malouda the ball in the danger zone. Torres took a quick pass and although he managed to keep possession, the space was closed down and he was crowded out as he drove towards goal.

On 31 minutes, Sturridge took possession out wide and as everyone was expecting the cross, he unleashed a surprise left-foot crack at the target. Leno had to react quickly to claw it away from the bottom corner of his net. It was looking like a moment of inspiration might be required to break down Leverkusen, although they weren't without mistakes in defence.

For a minute the game became one of counter-attacks, Malouda giving the ball away but Meireles' sliding challenge halted a dangerous run by Kiessling. David Luiz sent Chelsea on the attack but Torres' cross was well defended.

Castro was booked for reacting badly when a free-kick was given against the Leverkusen full-back as half-time approached and then Sturridge went close with a shot from outside the area after Meireles had taken a free-kick with Leverkusen unprepared.

With the last action of the half, Ivanovic headed a Mata free-kick but it was easy for the keeper to claim.

Second Half

Leverkusen started the second 45 minutes on top but when a Mikel clearing header dropped Ballack's way, he volleyed it high into the Shed Upper. It was not the end of the chances for the former midfielder of this parish.

Chelsea changed shape briefly, Mata playing behind Torres, and a great David Luiz pass got his side attacking again and the crowd going once more, but Leverkusen came back strongly.

Schurrle was able to find space in the area to drill a shot past the post and then, after Chelsea had lost the ball in our half, it was played forward to Ballack. The

34-year-old was suddenly in front of goal and had the best chance of the game so far, but Cech blocked as he so often does and the rebound fell safely.

That was not the end of the visitors' chances and now Cech was truly earning his keep, saving from Schurrle after another passing move through our defence.

Amongst all that Leverkusen attacking, Torres headed a Malouda cross firmly down but Leno saved it on the line.

Chelsea also hit woodwork before the goal eventually came. It was Sturridge's shot that proved too hot to handle and Leno scrambled it against the post.

The two managers began to make changes. Anelka and Lampard were introduced and Ballack's evening came to an end.

David Luiz's earlier booking for pulling back Schurrle had been long forgotten by the time he both began and finished the move that led to the breakthrough goal.

Driving forward into the German half, the Brazilian slipped the ball out to Cole and then was in position to take Torres' lay-off and dispatch the ball into the far bottom corner from the edge of the area. It was a sweet, sweet strike.

Mata's curler was creeping inside the post for a second goal soon after before Leno caught it with two hands, and the Spaniard fired on target again but this time the keeper tipped it over.

The chances were all Chelsea's in the closing stages, Lampard warming Leno's hands and a foul ruling out a goal when Anelka headed in.

With the final whistle just seconds away, Chelsea made the most of space down our left and Torres, with his second assist of the night, squared the ball for Mata to knock it past an exposed Leno.

Chelsea (4-3-3):
Cech (c); Bosingwa, Ivanovic, David Luiz (Alex 75), Cole; Meireles (Lampard 64), Mikel, Malouda; Sturridge (Anelka 64), Torres, Mata. **Unused subs:** Hilario, Ferreira, McEachran, Kalou. **Scorers:** David Luiz 66, Mata 90+2. **Booked:** Torres 8, David Luiz 58.

Bayer Leverkusen (4-2-3-1):
Leno; Castro, Reinartz, Toprak, Kadlec; Bender (Balitsch 79), Rolfes (c); Schürrle, Ballack (Augusto 65), Sam (Derdiyok 72); Kiessling. **Unused subs:** Yelldell, Friedrich, Bellarabi, Schwaab. **Booked:** Castro 38, Bender 71, Derdiyok 75.

Referee: Stephane Lannoy (France)
Attendance: 33,820.

"I think it was a game that was very well played by both teams. I think both teams wanted that first goal because it would give them the edge.

The second goal took its time to arrive and again there was always emotions in the game, both teams started feeling tired and losing control of a couple of tasks, and both teams were very driven emotionally, but eventually it fell for us in the last minute to give us 2-0."

Andre Villas-Boas

'It was a nice goal. Now I have three goals at Stamford Bridge and I am very happy. I love the atmosphere here, the support, and all the time the players are together and this is of big importance."

David Luiz

"We know this year with the quality we have in the squad there will be a big turnover. Every player plays internationals and we have a lot of games so to achieve our goals we know we have to be fresh and there is competition for places. Most important is the team and with that team spirit we can go very far."

Florent Malouda

49

VALENCIA V CHELSEA

Mestalla, 28.09.11

Juan Mata:

"My first game in the UEFA Champions League [was against Chelsea], now four years later I am going to play for Chelsea against Valencia. It will be strange to be in a different changing room. That will make it a special game and I know what the atmosphere is like in the Mestalla when Valencia play in this competition. I don't know yet if I will find it difficult – tomorrow I will find out – but I am going to focus on helping my team to win. I will say hello to all my old team-mates before the game but at kick-off, that is when friendship ends. After the game it will be different but during it every player must focus on helping his team to win."

Fernando Torres:

"It is a massive stadium with a very good atmosphere, I played with Atletico as an away team, but also as a home team with Spain, because we used to play there for important games three or four years back.

Before the game the stadium was completely full, even two hours before when we arrived on the bus the fans were waiting for us, so they gave us excellent support but it will be very hostile playing there as the away team, which is good for Valencia."

Valencia 1
(Soldado (pen) 86)

Chelsea 1
(Lampard 56)

Late penalty pegs Blues back...

Chelsea had to settle for a point at the Mestalla after a late penalty for Valencia cancelled out what looked set to be the winner by Frank Lampard.

Having won on our previous two trips to the Spanish club, both of which came in 2007, a repeat appeared to be on the cards when our incisive football finally delivered a goal shortly after half-time. The home side's goalkeeper, Diego Alves, had repelled everything thrown at him until Florent Malouda picked out an unmarked Lampard in the box for a trademark finish by the Blues No 8.

We continued to test the keeper after grabbing that deserved lead, but Valencia weren't going to go down without a fight and they were given a golden chance to grab an equaliser when Salomon Kalou handled in the area. The in-form Roberto Soldado scored and although Nicolas Anelka nearly won it late on, it was a point apiece.

Best moment...

53

On his first start in three games and following his manager answering numerous questions on the player in the pre-match press conference, Lampard was always going to be a good bet for first goal in this game. Although he made it look simple, the accuracy achieved with a first-time strike on a ball coming across the pitch was classic Lamps.

Team news

David Luiz, Frank Lampard and Florent Malouda returned to the Chelsea starting line-up. Branislav Ivanovic, Raul Meireles and Nicolas Anelka made way with Juan Mata moving to the right of the attack to accommodate Malouda on the left. Fernando Torres retained his place at centre-forward.

First Half

Valencia looked to have anything but a solid defence in the opening five minutes. First they gifted the ball to Fernando Torres in a dangerous area, then Malouda benefitted from similar generosity by Ever Banega and as he tried to thread the ball through the crowd to Ramires in the area, it was cleared for a corner that keeper Diego Alves punched away very unconvincingly.

Valencia put together a couple of promising moves with Sergio Canales at the heart of them but Petr Cech was able to deal with the end results before Chelsea broke from the back, David Luiz sending Ramires haring into their half. Having beaten one player, a great run was ended by a foul from centre-back Victor Ruiz who could have been judged last man by a harsher ref. Instead he was shown yellow and Chelsea didn't capitalise from the free-kick that Lampard hit too straight.

Chelsea survived a couple of Valencia corners midway through the half and although the home side were finding space with intelligent movement when they went forward, they weren't creating chances.

That was until Alba got forward from left-back with Ramires briefly off the field for treatment. His ball into the near post was struck first time by Soldado but thankfully into the side-netting. That was as close as either side came to scoring in the first 45 minutes.

Both sides enjoyed spells in possession and it needed Terry at his most defiant when centre-forward Soldado was threatening to find the room to shoot. Cech continued to gather speculative balls into his six-yard box.

Mata, who had been quiet on his return to the Mestalla, played one of the passes of the game so far as half-time approached, across the pitch to Cole who headed into what could have been the danger zone but for the lack of blue shirts.

Pablo Hernandez spun sharply and tested Cech from distance before the half came to a close but our keeper had not been truly tested by the interval, and Chelsea, in what looked our toughest fixture at the start of the group stage, could be satisfied with that.

Second Half

It was all about the Valencia keeper Diego Alves at the start of the second period. Firstly he pulled off a marvellous diving save to keep out Torres' firm header after Bosingwa's cross had found our No9 just six yards out. Then moments later he stood up and saved from Ramires who had used great pace to make the most of a Lampard pass.

The one-man defence continued with another save from Torres followed by a stop with his foot when Valencia defender Victor Ruiz could only divert a hard, low cross at his own goal.

There was, however, nothing Alves could do except stand rooted on 56 minutes when Malouda's right-foot ball across the box fell to Lampard, just inside the area,

and the vice-captain was unerring in his low finish, as he had been so many times before.

That had most certainly been coming although the Valencia threat had also been greater than in the first half, one slightly over-hit cross having a less-than-full Mestalla gasping, and Cech dealing well with an angled shot with the game still scoreless.

Later in the half, Terry was in place to clear when Cech had left his goal to address danger and had been bypassed by a cross. Cech did very well on 70 minutes to save from substitute Piatti and Chelsea escaped when Rami planted a header just wide when a cross cleared David Luiz.

Cech saved again from Fegholi and Piatti shot wide with Valencia knowing they were only 15 minutes from defeat and piling on the pressure.

Chelsea could have eased it by scoring a killer goal when Lampard teed up Malouda but his low shot was saveable.

Cech's best save of the game came with just five minutes left on the clock, a full-length effort from Jonas' sweetly struck shot, but the deserved clean sheet was not to arrive. Substitute Kalou, who had not been long on the pitch, was judged to have handled when a corner was delivered into a crowd. He might have been pushed, but Soldado converted the penalty.

With 89 minutes on the clock, it was Anelka's turn to be kept out by Diego Alves who saved from close range with his leg.

At the final whistle, Cole and Mata picked up bookings for protesting that a free-kick had not been allowed to be taken. It was a night when a point was not a bad return, but we could have easily taken more.

Valencia (4-2-3-1):
D Alves; Miguel, Rami, Víctor Ruiz, Jordi Alba; Albelda, Éver (Jonas 72); Pablo (Feghouli 72), Canales, Mathieu (Piatti 58); Soldado. **Unused subs:** Guaita, Bruno Saltor, Maduro, Parejo. **Scorer:** Soldado pen 86. **Booked:** Victor Ruiz 12, Albelda 46.

Chelsea (4-3-3):
Cech; Bosingwa, D Luiz, Terry (c), Cole; Ramires (Meireles 65), Mikel, Lampard (Kalou 82); Mata, Torres (Anelka 72), Malouda. **Unused subs:** Turnbull, Ivanovic, Romeu, Drogba. **Scorer:** Lampard 56. **Booked:** Kalou 86, Malouda 90+2, Mata 90+3, Cole 90+3.

Referee: Nicola Rizzoli (Italy)
Attendance: 33,791

"It was a sweet moment, the season hasn't quite got going for me yet for a few reasons, so to come here in a game like this and score a goal is the start of a big season for me.

Qualification games in the group stage can be slightly bland at times but this was more exciting. You have to find a middle ground of protecting your lead and playing attractive stuff. From our point of view it was a good performance although disappointing to lose that lead.

They're a fantastic team, we watched the video from when they played Barcelona a couple of weeks ago and we out-Barcelona'd Barcelona in a way, played great football and we were very aware of what they could do tonight. We sat back a bit after the goal, you know against a team of quality you're going to suffer at some points, and probably a draw was a fair result."

Frank Lampard

"The performance was solid and a draw away from home, if it was proposed to you before the game you would take it, but it leaves you with a strange feeling because we were so near a win.

But a draw leaves us in a good position in the group. We are still leaders and looking forward to the Genk games because if we take six points from those then we almost certainly qualify."

Andre Villas-Boas

CHELSEA V GENK

Stamford Bridge, 19.10.11

Petr Cech:

"It is not easy when you come as a big player to a new environment and a different team and [Juan Mata] has settled brilliantly.

Creating goal-scoring opportunities is why we brought him and is exactly what he is doing. He has been brilliant so far and I hope he stays fit and is going to be playing the same way."

John Terry:

"The group stages will give you one really tough game nine times out of 10 because the way the seedings work, but you always come up against good opposition nowadays. With that in mind if you can win your home games it will serve you well.

There are teams on paper that you should go and beat but away from home these can be difficult places to go because of the weather or pitches, so if you can look after yourself at home, as we have done in recent years, then you should be alright.

Until now we've always done well in the group stages, we've never failed to go through and we tend to get ourselves in the right position early on."

61

Chelsea 5
(Meireles 7, Torres 10, 26, Ivanovic 41, Kalou 71)

Genk 0

Five-star Blues in record win...

Chelsea recorded our biggest win in a UEFA Champions League game at Stamford Bridge as Belgian champions Genk were on the receiving end of a five-goal drubbing.

The Blues could have been in front shortly after the kick-off as Fernando Torres hit the post when well placed, but we didn't have to wait much longer for the opener as Raul Meireles fired in a long-range effort for his first goal for the club.

Undeterred by his earlier miss, Torres capitalised on a precise through ball by Lampard to double our lead before superbly heading in Meireles' cross to make it 3-0. And our lead was four by the interval, as Branislav Ivanovic got his head to Florent Malouda's free-kick to leave the keeper with no chance.

There was to be no hat-trick for Torres in the second half, but it was from the rebound of his shot that substitute Salomon Kalou steered home his first of the season to round off the scoring.

63

Best moment...

While Fernando Torres may have been disappointed not to have walked away with the match ball, his first-half brace was a cause for celebration.

Team news

Fernando Torres was supported in attack by the French pair of Nicolas Anelka and Florent Malouda. David Luiz returned in place of John Terry and Oriol Romeu played his first Champions League game in place of John Mikel Obi. Raul Meireles came in for the injured Ramires.

First Half

Fernando Torres created the first opportunity of the game in the third minute with a fantastic turn which left two Genk defenders in his wake on the halfway line, before he found Malouda out wide, but the Frenchman's delivery was turned behind for a corner.

Only minutes later the Spaniard could have put the Blues in front, when he was put through by a fantastic flighted ball from Raul Meireles, but Torres could only nudge his effort onto the post.

Chelsea weren't to be denied a minute later, though, when a sublime Meireles effort from just outside the Genk box flew beyond the stranded Laszlo Koteles into the bottom corner to give the Portuguese midfielder his first goal for the Blues.

Four minutes later and the lead was doubled when Torres, intelligently played in by captain for the night Frank Lampard, finished in trademark fashion for his first goal in the competition since he netted against the Blues for Liverpool in the 2008/09 quarter-final at Anfield.

Twenty-year-old Romeu, making his first start in the UEFA Champions League for Chelsea, was showing no sign of nerves in central midfield, orchestrating things effortlessly with a combination of tough tackling and simple, efficient passing. Florent Malouda, so instrumental down the left in the opening exchanges, should have made it 3-0 in the 22nd minute but he could only steer Torres' cross just past the post.

The Spaniard had his second of the night and Chelsea's third a minute later, expertly getting in front of his man to head home from an exquisite Meireles cross from wide on the right.

The midfield trio of Romeu, Lampard and Meireles were completely running the show, and the injury-ravaged Belgians had no answer for the pass-and-move style of play.

Lampard almost made it 4-0 just after the half-hour mark only to see his header from Torres' cross narrowly miss the target.

David Luiz was then on the receiving end of a crunching tackle, before dusting himself down and taking the resulting free-kick, but the flamboyant Brazilian's effort was comfortably saved.

Genk, to their credit, refused to cave in, but their rare attacks often broke down in the final third before they had a chance to test the virtual spectator Petr Cech in the Chelsea goal.

Five minutes before the break, a fantastic counter-attack involving Torres and Lampard came to nothing when Nicolas Anelka shot wide from just inside the penalty area when he should really have done better.

It was 4-0, however, a minute later when Branislav Ivanovic rose above the sloppy Genk defence to head home Malouda's free-kick to end the game as a contest.

Second Half

With the upcoming west London derby against QPR in mind, Villas-Boas replaced Ashley Cole with Paulo Ferreira at the break, making full use of his favoured rotation policy and giving fringe players some much-needed game time.

Some neat interplay between Bosingwa and Anelka down the right-hand side almost resulted in a chance two minutes after the restart but the veteran forward's inviting delivery was turned behind for a corner.

Thomas Buffel had the visitors' first real sight of goal when he found himself unmarked at the far post, but he dithered on the ball and found his weak effort blocked by Ivanovic.

Torres opted for the spectacular in the 53rd minute when he attempted to turn and volley a floated pass from the technically-gifted Luiz, but his impressive attempt didn't quite come off. Malouda should have scored soon after when he was clean through on goal, but his effort was easily stopped by Koteles.

Lampard was then penalised for his honesty in the 58th minute after attempting to stay on his feet when he was clearly fouled in the Genk penalty area. The Blues were again dominating possession but, unlike in the first-half, they lacked a cutting-edge in front of goal.

Jose Bosingwa then tested the palms of Koteles with a stinging effort from distance, but the keeper was equal to it, before Villas-Boas made his second change of the night, replacing Lampard with Salomon Kalou.

The Ivorian striker had to wait only four minutes for his first goal of the season, reacting first and finishing from close range, after Koteles had denied Torres his hat-trick.

Alex then went close with a trademark free-kick from distance with practically his first touch of the ball, but his effort fizzed wide of the post.

As the game petered out into what amounted to little more than a glorified training session for the home side, Malouda met a pinpoint Ferreira cross from out wide on the left, but his header sailed high over the crossbar.

Chelsea (4-3-3):
Cech; Bosingwa (Alex 77), Ivanovic, David Luiz, Cole (Ferreira h/t); Meireles, Romeu, Lampard (c)(Kalou 67); Anelka, Torres, Malouda. **Subs not used:** Turnbull, Mikel, Mata, Sturridge. **Scorers:** Meireles 7, Torres 10, 26, Ivanovic 41, Kalou 71. **Booked:** David Luiz 16.

Genk: (4-4-2):
Koteles; Ngcongca, Masuero (Camus h/t), Tozser (c), Pudil; Buffel, Vanden Borre, Hyland, De Bruyne; Vossen (Nwanganga 80), Barda (Ndabashinze 70). **Subs not used:** Sandomierski, Derwael, Limbombe, Ogunjimi. **Booked:** Hyland 14, Pudil 41.

Referee: Aleksei Nikolaev (Russia)
Attendance: 38,518

"A 5-0 win shows how we dominated the game. We controlled the game for 90 minutes and we had some chances to score more but unfortunately we didn't.

Fernando had a great performance today. He worked very hard in training and this is a result of how he is working. We're looking for him to be better and better.

It is a normal thing that players need time when they change clubs. Now everything is perfect and we're looking forward."

Branislav Ivanovic

"It's always good to come in and score, it gives you confidence and I am pleased with that performance.

We scored early and that's important because it means you get more space to create chances. We have a good squad and if you want to do well in the UEFA Champions League you have to have a good bench. Some players were left out tonight but we were still able to put in a good performance.

It's good to have Fernando at his top level and you need that if you are going to go a long way."

Salomon Kalou

GENK V CHELSEA

Cristal Arena, 02.11.11

Branislav Ivanovic:

"We know how to play and will do everything to be strong defensively. We have to be fully concentrated for the whole game and be strong for 90 minutes."

Salomon Kalou:

"We need to approach this game like we did the first match against them. When you play against teams like that you have to kill the game early, like we did do, otherwise they can gain confidence and it becomes harder to break them down."

71

Genk 1
(Vossen 60)

Chelsea 1
(Ramires 25)

Genk grab their chance...

Chelsea were held to a draw by Genk, with a missed penalty costing us as the hosts fought their way back into our Group E clash.

It had all looked so straightforward when Ramires had advanced through a static home defence to fire Chelsea into a 25th-minute lead, an advantage that could have been doubled when David Luiz took responsibility before the break, the Brazilian's spot-kick saved by Genk goalkeeper Laszlo Koteles.

The miss would come back to haunt the Blues on the hour mark when striker Jelle Vossen levelled from close range to earn his side an unlikely point.

The introduction of Frank Lampard to central midfield shortly after Genk's goal handed the initiative back to the Blues but, ultimately a Chelsea winner proved elusive.

Team news

73

There was one change to the Chelsea line-up from the home game against Genk. Ramires came in for Frank Lampard.

David Luiz partnered Branislav Ivanovic in central defence and there was another start for Oriol Romeu as the anchor midfielder. Raul Meireles played on the left of midfield.

John Terry and Frank Lampard were both on the bench.

Genk's Brazilian defender Nadson, out injured a fortnight ago, returned and ◉

Fabien Camus came into the Belgian midfield. There was also a change up front where Kennedy Nwanganga partnered Jelle Vossen.

First Half

In spite of their 5-0 thrashing at Stamford Bridge a fortnight earlier, Genk started the game playing the better football but visibly lacked the killer edge.

While Meireles sat in the centre, his midfield partner galloped forward and it was Ramires who would open the scoring for Chelsea after 25 minutes, taking control of a loose ball after some sloppy Genk play and driving on, exchanging passes with Torres before shooting low through the legs of the keeper from a tight angle.

As at the Bridge, the Belgians had created their own problems, and they nearly worsened on the half-hour when Torres flashed an effort just wide from 25 yards, and Ramires headed a Cole cross wide of the post.

An exquisite move involving Cole and Meireles sent Malouda into the area with space to pick his pass, but his Torres-bound ball was cut out by Khaleem Hyland, who had to hold his breath to see the ball drop wide of the post for a corner. Villas-Boas's side were in complete control as half-time approached.

Malouda attempted a cross but at close quarters the ball struck Thomas Buffel's arm – penalty to Chelsea. David Luiz stepped up confidently and struck cleanly, but Koteles guessed correctly and palmed the ball away low to his right.

Second Half

Genk's Kevin De Bruyne scuffed a decent chance five minutes after the break, following patient right to left build-up from the home side.

Cech had to dive bravely at the feet of Kennedy Nwanganga to preserve Chelsea's lead a couple of minutes later with the ball bouncing around the away side's penalty area.

A couple of corners had the home fans in the mood as they willed their side forward once more, and their reward would arrive on the hour.

Fabien Camus, absent at the Bridge, strode into the area down Chelsea's right and pulled back into the danger area where forward Jelle Vossen stroked the ball beyond Cech and into the net.

Villas-Boas rang the changes with 25 minutes remaining, introducing Lampard and Daniel Sturridge for Ramires and Anelka.

Whether it was the shock of conceding or the changes brought by the manager, Chelsea began to wrestle control back from the hosts and Meireles could have headed us back into the lead when he met a Malouda cross, instead heading straight at the goalkeeper.

Lampard had an opportunity on 78 minutes when Sturridge ploughed into the box and crossed low, although the midfielder couldn't make contact with the ball.

At the other end Cech had to advance off his line again to stop substitute Anthony Limbombe sliding Genk into an unlikely lead after De Bruyne had weighted a smart pass through the channel, but as the clock ticked over the 90-minute mark it was Malouda who could have snatched a win for the visitors.

The Frenchman did everything right, lifting the ball over Koteles from the tightest of angles, but between them the two covering defenders managed to scramble the ball behind for only a corner.

It was the last chance in a game Chelsea felt should have been won, but could still have lost.

Genk (4-4-2):
Koteles; Vanden Borre, Hyland, Nadson, Ngcongca; Buffel (Ndabashinze 68), Camus, Tozser (c), De Bruyne; Vossen (Barda 86), Nwanganga (Limbombe 81).
Unused subs: Sandomierski, Sarr, Durwael, Ofori-Appiah. **Goals:** Vossen 60.
Booked: De Bruyne 75.

75

Chelsea (4-3-3):
Cech (c); Bosingwa, Ivanovic, David Luiz, Cole; Ramires (Lampard 65), Romeu (Mata 76), Meireles; Anelka (Sturridge 65), Torres, Malouda. **Unused subs:** Turnbull, Terry, McEachran, Kalou. **Goals:** Ramires 25. **Booked:** Meireles 90.

Referee: Svein Oddvar Moen (Norway)
Attendance: 22,584

"Genk played in this game a little bit like the second half at Stamford Bridge. They didn't want to concede a lot of goals like they did in the first half at Stamford Bridge and they were really compact and they were difficult to play against. But we had the possession and we had more chances but the crowd and the atmosphere could help them in some situations and they played a very good game. The most difficult thing in football is to create chances. After you can always talk about efficiency and that is a matter of confidence, but the basics are there in our play. We had the possession of the ball, we played well and of course the bad thing is we have conceded another goal, but we still created chances so if we change and be more clinical then the positive results will be back. I would be more worried if we couldn't create chances. Of course it is a bad moment because we don't have the result we expected and our ambition is very high but there is no reason to be in doubt and be negative."

Florent Malouda

"It's not a bad result away from home but we expected to win. I wouldn't say we lost control. We were quite organised in the first half and in the second half I think we shouldn't confuse losing control of the game with emotions coming from the stadium. Genk made the most of a couple of opportunities they had, one went in and it finished 1-1."

Andre Villas-Boas

77

BAYER LEVERKUSEN V CHELSEA

BayArena, 23.11.11

Andre Villas-Boas:

"We have an extremely good opportunity to qualify. A win is what we are seeking with all our strengths.

Two draws in the last two games will qualify us but it is not what we are looking for. What we have set out to do this season is to take the initiative in every game and try to win every game and it won't be any different against Bayer Leverkusen."

Juan Mata:

"From today we have to start a new objective, to win in Germany, to qualify for the next round. It is like a final for us because Bayer Leverkusen is close behind and we need the three points.

We have to be a compact team, play together, do what we know to do because we are still a very good team with very good players, and we have to show that together on the pitch."

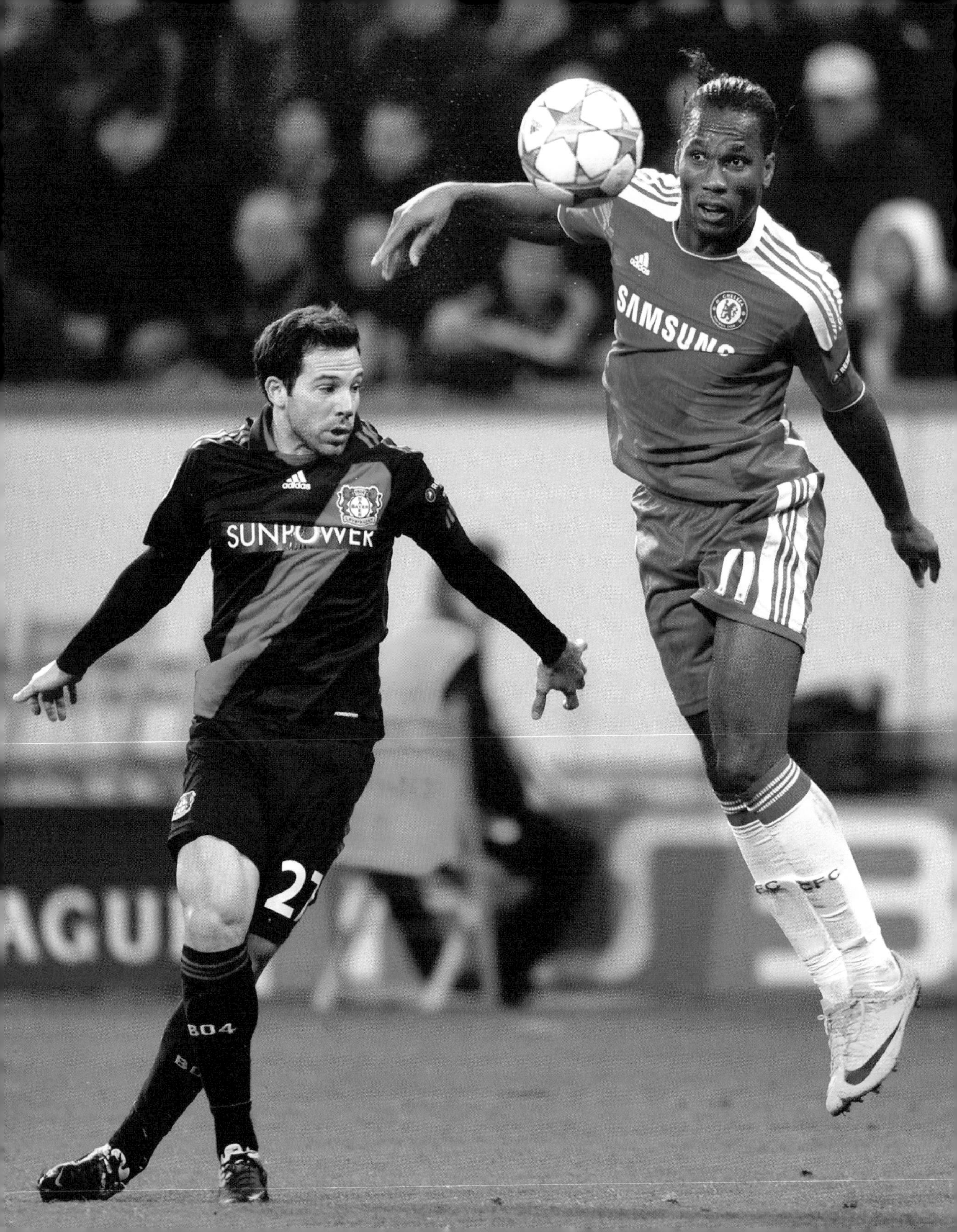
SAMSUNG
SUNPOWER
adidas
adidas
B04

Bayer Leverkusen 2
(Derdiyok 72, Friedrich 90)

Chelsea 1
(Drogba 47)

Late Bayer strike leaves group in balance

Defeat to Bayer Leverkusen meant the Blues required a victory or a goalless draw against Valencia in the final group game to book a spot in the knockout phase after a last-minute goal condemned us to an undeserved defeat in Germany.

Following an uneventful first half, the Blues went ahead just three minutes after the restart through Didier Drogba. The Ivorian collected a lofted through-ball from Daniel Sturridge and, despite appearing to have lost the ball, a neat bit of skill gave him a shooting lane – and, as expected, he took full advantage of it.

However, the Bundesliga side drew level when substitute Eren Derdiyok made an immediate impact, heading home just two minutes after coming off the bench. And another header proved to be our undoing in stoppage time as Manuel Friedrich rose highest in the box to head home from a corner.

Team news

Didier Drogba started for the first time in the UEFA Champions League this season, flanked by Daniel Sturridge and Juan Mata. Ashley Cole was missing after suffering an ankle injury in training. Jose Bosingwa was asked to play left-back, Branislav Ivanovic was on the right and John Terry and David Luiz made up the rest of the defence. Raul Meireles replaced John Mikel Obi as the anchor midfielder.

Bayer Leverkusen made four changes from the side that lost at Stamford Bridge, three of them in defence where only Michal Kadlec remained. Castro came in on the right of midfield. Michael Ballack, wearing a protective face mask similar to Petr Cech's, also started.

First Half

Leverkusen had the early territorial advantage but with little menace to their attack.

On 12 minutes Sturridge escaped into space in the box and hammered the ball square but Leno in the home goal caught well.

There was an interruption just past the quarter-of-an-hour mark when David Luiz went down hurt having challenged for an aerial ball that had come back off Bosingwa. The stretcher came on but wasn't needed as the Brazilian walked off the pitch for treatment. He continued soon after.

The cagey start to the game continued past the halfway mark in the first period. Chelsea won a free-kick over 30 yards from goal but Lampard's ambitious attempt had too much height on it.

Chelsea's first shot on target came in the 29th minute – a Drogba free-kick but it was comfortable for the keeper.

Three minutes later Chelsea were far more concerned when Ballack got to a corner first and from close range, headed against the bar. The former Chelsea midfielder's aerial prowess was not diminished.

The home side's centre-forward Kiessling had been losing out to Terry in the physical contest so far and when he dropped deeper, his foul on Bosingwa earned him a booking.

It had been an even contest for a while but as half-time approached there was the promising sign of Chelsea finishing the half the stronger side.

Drogba had the best Chelsea chance so far when he was put through on the right side of the area by a touch of Sturridge class but from out wide the Ivorian shot over.

Then with three minutes remaining Sturridge held the ball in an advanced position, allowing Mata the chance to shoot but without the power to beat the keeper. That was another presentable chance. Chelsea moved forward quickly once more and after Lampard had been halted in front of goal, Sturridge tried to curl one in from distance but Leno claimed.

Late on Ballack was shown a yellow card for dissent, Kadlec having earlier gone in the book to make it 3-0 on cautions at the interval.

Second Half

Drogba may not have made the most of it the first time Sturridge had set him up with an opening but he was making no mistake second time. In possession with his back to goal 15 yards out, he was initially well policed but then turned inside in trademark style and found the bottom corner.

Ivanovic then tried to hammer home the advantage but his shot from distance was too straight, The Serbian then became Chelsea's first booked player for a foul on Sam.

For a minute just before the hour, the game turned into a duel between the two masked men, first Cech tipping over at full stretch after an adept bicycle kick by Ballack, and then when the same player got on the end of a ball into the six-yard

box, it looked for all the world a goal but Cech somehow parried from point-blank range.

There was an escape soon after as substitute Schurrle headed straight into the Chelsea keeper's arms.

It was a strong few minutes by Bayer but when Terry cleared a Ballack cross, Sturridge was able to use his pace to run from his own half past his marker. He made space outside the last defender but couldn't then beat the keeper.

Malouda and Alex were introduced in quick succession, Mata and David Luiz making way. Bayer made a change too, Derdiyok coming on and it paid off almost immediately for the home team.

Sam was the player who was found in space on the left and with Cech exposed and covering the potential shot, the winger chipped the ball over to Derdiyok at the far post who headed in. There were 72 minutes played.

Drogba thought he should have had a penalty when he was tumbled in the box as Chelsea looked for a response but there was nothing given. The game was very much in the balance.

It looked to be opening up for Chelsea when Malouda floated a ball over to Drogba who was not tightly marked but he volleyed wide. Instead it was the home side who snatched it as stoppage time began. From a corner, Friedrich got above Alex on the penalty spot to head in off the underside of the bar.

Leverkusen (4-2-3-1):
Leno; Schwaab (Schürrle 56), Friedrich, Toprak, Kadlec (Derdiyok 70); Bender, Rolfes (c); Castro, Ballack, Sam; Kiessling (Oczipka 81). **Scorer:** Derdiyok 72, Friedrich 90. **Unused subs:** Giefer, Reinartz, Ortega, Jørgensen. **Booked:** Kiessling 35, Kadlec 39, Ballack 43.

Chelsea (4-3-3):
Cech; Ivanovic, D Luiz (Alex 68), Terry (c), Bosingwa; Ramires, Meireles (Mikel 79); Sturridge, Lampard, Mata (Malouda 65); Drogba **Unused subs:** Turnbull, McEachran, Kalou, Torres. **Scorer:** Drogba 47. **Booked:** Ivanovic 54, Meireles 71.

Referee: Viktor Kassai (Hungary)
Attendance: 29,285

"This result changes the nature of the group, and now we go to the final match against Valencia to decide our fate. Valencia are a team on the up in terms of results, and we will need Stamford Bridge fully behind us in order to find the right intensity, but it is in our hands and we expect to do our job. It's our responsibility and we don't want to let the fans down. We believe a lot in the players' talent, and they believe in us as well. When you are experiencing a run of results as we are now, we go into every little detail and try to get them right, and we just have to continue to work, and believe that the win is close."

Andre Villas-Boas

"The difference [between the sides] was we scored two and Chelsea scored one and I think a draw would have been fair. It was a big victory for us but we believed in it every minute and we could feel that Chelsea is not in their strongest moment. When the score was 1-0 to Chelsea I knew that it would be difficult to come back and scoring from the corner in the last minute, it was a little bit lucky. Chelsea should believe because they have big players, they have experienced players and I am sure they know what they can do. If you don't get the results it is always difficult, I know this from the past, but you have to fight and then the victories will come back."

Michael Ballack

87

CHELSEA V VALENCIA

Stamford Bridge, 06.12.11

Didier Drogba:

"These are the kind of games you want to play in. It is similar to all the big games we have played in the UEFA Champions League like the quarter-final and semi-finals against Liverpool – games when there was a lot of tension.

You can feel that everybody is concentrating 200 per cent and I love that kind of emotion on the pitch.

This is a new challenge, we have all had other challenges before and this is a new one, and I am ready to attack it. It is a difficult moment and we have to stick together. We all have bad moments but if you stick together the good things will come."

Daniel Sturridge:

"The mood in the camp has been great, everybody is bubbling and playing with a smile on their face. We know we can win this game.

The players we have in our squad are used to playing in big games. They've played in UEFA Champions League Finals and semi-finals, etc.

Every game at this level is difficult because you are playing against the best teams in Europe. It will be no different this time, of course, but we will be going into the game to win it because we need to."

89

Chelsea 3
(Drogba 2, 75, Ramires 21)

Valencia 0

Drogba double sends Blues through

What was all the fuss about? Chelsea eased through to the last 16 of the UEFA Champions League after a brilliant home win, with goals courtesy of Didier Drogba and Ramires.

It had all looked so dangerous before the game, with victory needed to guarantee qualification, but nerves were quickly settled when after two minutes Drogba had put us in front. He danced around a defender inside the box and smashed low into the bottom corner. The same player turned creator for the second when he sent Ramires through, though the goal owed as much to the midfielder's persistence in chasing a speculative through ball as it did the slide-rule pass in behind the defence.

It was not all plain sailing though, as in between Valencia struck a post and Petr Cech pulled off a world-class save to deny David Albelda an equaliser, but Chelsea rarely looked threatened afterwards. Drogba rolled in a third 15 minutes from time to make three huge points safe, and the Stamford Bridge party could begin.

91

Best moment...

A minute after netting the third, Drogba was withdrawn to huge applause around the Bridge having turned in one of his best displays in memory, a performance quickly acknowledged to the 33-year-old by every member of Chelsea's backroom team and substitutes.

Team news

Raul Meireles replaced Frank Lampard while Didier Drogba led the forward line with Daniel Sturridge and Juan Mata the wide players. Jose Bosingwa was unavailable.

First Half

Andre Villas-Boas and his men knew a win would guarantee a place in the last 16, but anything else would throw qualification into serious doubt.

A goalless draw would suffice provided Genk did not beat Bayer Leverkusen in the group's other game, but a score draw would see Chelsea eliminated on goals scored to the benefit of our Spanish opposition.

If ever there was cause for nerves, this was it, yet it was the visitors who succumbed to the pressure. Inside three minutes Valencia had given the ball away needlessly four times, and after Meireles had tested Diego Alves with a bending effort, we went in front through Drogba.

Daniel Sturridge nicked the ball inside the Valencia half and crossed deep to Mata, who brought the ball down and pulled it back for the forward to control and fire home with his left foot into the far corner.

Valencia were quickly on the lookout for an equaliser though, and before five minutes were up they had struck the woodwork when attacking left-back Jordi Alba broke into the Chelsea box and cracked an effort against Petr Cech's near post.

Minutes later David Albelda, the captain, had produced a stunning drive from range destined for the top corner until Cech extended every inch of his 6ft 5ins frame to tip it behind for a corner.

There had not yet been time to pause for breath and this was perhaps just as well, because when respite did come the vulnerability of Chelsea's position came immediately to mind. One Valencia goal would still knock us out.

There was enough experience in this Chelsea side to stand strong though, Cech had done his bit, John Terry was clearing everything inside the box, and then Drogba created a second, killer goal.

The Ivorian showed pace and power to run at the away defence before adding a

little guile too, slipping a ball through for Ramires in behind the defence, and while defender Victor Ruiz was favourite, the Brazilian had the determination to succeed, got round his man and slotted it calmly beyond Diego Alves. This had been the perfect start, with 21 minutes on the clock.

Sturridge had a right-footed drive pushed around the post and Meireles flashed one wide. At the other end Tino Costa drove two yards off target with Chelsea looking comfortable despite Valencia enjoying the majority of possession.

The Blues went in at the break looking in complete control, though Villas-Boas will have warned that one slip would allow Valencia straight back into contention.

Second Half

The second half came to life when Romeu set Sturridge away on a counter-attack after winning the ball on the edge of his own box, and having skinned his marker, Sturridge forced Diego Alves into a decent stop at his near post.

Cech was called into action when Sofiane Feghouli broke into the box but the keeper was on fine form and able to palm the shot away, before defensive reinforcement arrived in the form of John Mikel Obi who replaced Ramires in midfield. He would sit deep alongside Romeu, allowing Meireles to go foraging further forward in what effectively became a 4-2-3-1.

Valencia still searched but it was Drogba came close to netting to kill the contest. Sturridge produced some classy footwork and sent the forward away in a tussle with a defender, but under pressure, dragged wide across goal.

Even at that stage, with a little under 20 minutes still to play, it did not look like mattering too much. Then, when Drogba went through once more, he made it absolutely sure, rolling the ball calmly beyond Diego Alves after Mata had been gifted the ball in dangerous territory.

Moments later Drogba departed the field, with Torres on in his place, to rapturous applause from an adoring Stamford Bridge.

Cech had to palm away an Aritz Aduriz header and clutch onto a Pablo Hernandez drive as the minutes ticked away, but the win was never in doubt and the Blues go marching into the knockout rounds.

Chelsea (4-3-3):
Cech; Ivanovic, David Luiz, Terry (c), Cole; Ramires (Mikel 64), Romeu, Meireles; Sturridge, Drogba (Torres 77), Mata (Malouda 82). **Unused subs:** Turnbull, Ferreira, Lampard, Kalou.
Goals: Drogba 2, 75, Ramires 21. **Booked:** Romeu 67.

Valencia (4-2-3-1):
Diego Alves; Barragan, Rami, Victor Ruiz, Jordi Alba (Aduriz 54); Tino Costa (Parejo 75), Albelda (c); Feghouli (Pablo Hernandez 64), Jonas, Mathieu; Soldado. **Unused subs:** Guaita, Mehmet Topal, Piatti, Dealber. **Booked:** Tino Costa 68.

Referee: Gianluca Rocchi (Italy)
Attendance: 41,109

"There was a lot of pressure but we still had a chance to finish top and we were positive – pressure can sometimes be positive. It was a good result and we qualified top of the group, we won 3-0 and scored a few goals so it was a good night for us and I am very happy. We needed to be compact because they scored seven goals [in their previous UEFA Champions League match against Genk] and were in good form, and I was impressed with the way we defended."

Didier Drogba

"It wasn't easy because it was a very tough game. The difference was that we took our chances and scored an early goal and it made a difference. In our previous games we didn't kill those teams off and here we had to fight until the end, but 3-0 is a very good result."

Petr Cech

"We left it late in the group but we did the job and Didier was fantastic for us. We knew it was going to be difficult, which it was, and we needed a big man to hold it up and give us time to get up, which he did. It was important we didn't concede. We set out with a game plan, and obviously the early goal from Didier helped us but we still had to hold on and the second goal came. The manager stressed that a third goal kills them off, which it did."

John Terry

97

NAPOLI V CHELSEA

Stadio San Paolo, 21.02.12

Didier Drogba:

"If Napoli is here it is because they deserve it. It's a fantastic place to play football. When I was young I was always looking at videos of Napoli and Maradona, so I am very happy to be here and we want to play this game and make a good impact."

Juan Mata:

"If we can score it will be very important. In a knockout tournament like this with two legs, the away goal is so important and so we will try to do that against Napoli on Tuesday."

99

Napoli 3
(Lavezzi 37, 64 Cavani 45+1)

Chelsea 1
(Mata 26)

Blues left with tough Italian job

Chelsea were left needing to overturn a two-goal deficit in the second leg of this UEFA Champions League last 16 tie after slipping to a 3-1 defeat against Napoli.

In an end-to-end game, the Blues drew first blood after a one-touch passing move resulted in Paolo Cannavaro slicing the ball up in the air, allowing Juan Mata to nonchalantly side-foot the ball beyond the reach of Morgan De Sanctis.

However, our advantage was wiped out by the half-time interval, as Ezequiel Lavezzi curled an unstoppable shot past Petr Cech and Edinson Cavani struck just before half-time when he bundled the ball in from close range.

Chelsea started the second half brightly and were looking the most likely side to score next, only for another Lavezzi strike on the counter-attack to put the game out of our reach. But with 90 minutes still to play at the Bridge, the tie was far from over...

Team news

101

John Terry was missing but Didier Drogba started for the first time since the Africa Cup of Nations.

Jose Bosingwa was at left-back with Branislav Ivanovic continuing on the right, while Ashley Cole was on the bench.

Ramires and Raul Meireles played deep in midfield with Juan Mata ahead of them and Daniel Sturridge and Florent Malouda the wide players.

First Half

Gary Cahill, making his UEFA Champions League debut, had to be alert to cut out a clever Lavezzi reverse pass in the second minute and shortly afterwards Petr Cech was quick off his line to punch clear with the diminutive Argentine giving chase.

It was the other South American that brought the first proper save from the Chelsea man, however. Cavani the Uruguayan was found in space by Swiss midfielder Gokhan Inler, and with time to bring the ball down and pick his spot fired fairly straight and low, Cech blocking well with his feet.

Shortly afterwards Bosingwa required treatment and was forced to withdraw. On in his place came Ashley Cole with only 11 minutes on the clock.

After Walter Gargano won possession and fed Lavezzi, who in turn played in an offside Cavani, it looked as though the hosts were going to carve open the visitors at will and Maggio brought another cat-like stop from Cech. Chelsea were still getting forward and finding spaces, but it was Napoli carrying all the threat, so imagine the surprise when Chelsea went in front before the half-hour.

A hurried move ended with Sturridge sending a loose pass into the home side's area, where Napoli captain Paolo Cannavaro scuffed his clearance to allow Juan Mata the opportunity to side-foot his volley home from 10 yards.

In the 10 minutes following the goal, Napoli failed to fashion any more chances, and the Blues, went close through a David Luiz header from Mata's corner. That chance came about after a Daniel Sturridge break. He attempted to find an unmarked Mata, but just failed with his delivery.

But, just when Villas-Boas' men may have been gaining confidence, Lavezzi struck, turning on the edge of the box and sending two Chelsea men the wrong way before curling neatly into the bottom corner beyond Cech.

Wounded, Chelsea came back and Ramires found himself with a decent chance almost immediately, but fired over with his left foot. The midfielder would have been ruing his miss by half-time, as it was he who had conceded the throw-in that eventually led to Napoli's second goal.

The ball was eventually worked from left to right where the cross was not prevented, and nor would it be cut out in flight, allowing Cavani the simplest of bundled finishes at the far post.

Second Half

Four minutes into the second period Napoli's defence almost contrived to give us another slice of luck, a low corner diverted goalwards but cleared off the line before we could claim an equaliser.

Dider Drogba, Mata and Florent Malouda linked up to force a save from De Sanctis, yet, at the other end, Napoli were still stringing together incisive passes and our defence was dealing with a great deal of pressure.

The task became a lot harder on 64 minutes as the hosts doubled their advantage. David Luiz was beaten by Cavani following a long ball from Campagnaro, and the forward then squared the ball to Lavezzi, taking an advanced Cech out of the game and allowing the Argentine to sweep home his second goal of the evening.

Andre Villas-Boas called for Lampard and Essien, replacements with experience aplenty. With Meireles and Malouda withdrawn, Chelsea switched to a diamond midfield, with Mata at its head, and Sturridge joined Drogba in attack. With men committed forward, though, we were more open at the back.

Another Napoli break saw the ball squared by Marek Hamsik and Maggio poke towards goal, only for Cole to be covering with a two-footed clearance right on the line. It was an intervention that may just have kept us alive.

Drogba turned over on the stroke of 90 minutes and Lampard saw a long-range effort held by De Sanctis as we pushed for a late goal to tighten things up, but there was no breakthrough and we returned home needing a sizeable, but not impossible, victory.

Napoli (3-4-2-1):
De Sanctis; Campagnaro, Cannavaro (c), Aronica; Maggio, Inler, Gargano, Zuniga; Hamsik (Pandev 81), Lavezzi (Dzemaili 73); Cavani. **Unused subs:** Rosati, Grava, Dossena, Fernandez, Britos. **Goals:** Lavezzi 37, 64 Cavani 45+1. **Booked:** Cavani 39.

Chelsea (4-2-3-1):
Cech; Ivanovic, Cahill, David Luiz, Bosingwa (Cole 11); Ramires, Meireles (Essien 69); Sturridge, Mata, Malouda (Lampard 69); Drogba (c). **Unused subs:** Turnbull, Mikel, Kalou, Torres. **Goals:** Mata 26. **Booked:** Meireles 40, Cahill 55.

Referee: Carlos Velasco Carballo (Spain)
Attendance: 52,495

"Napoli is a very strong, very intensive team in their stadium and, for sure, their supporters help them a lot. But, now, we have the second game and we are going to put 100 per cent in at the Bridge to win."

Juan Mata

"We have a two-goal disadvantage to overcome, but we are still in it and we will fight."

Petr Cech

"One of the small but good things to come out of that game is the away goal, which gives us a chance to believe. One of the most important things is to not concede a goal at Stamford Bridge as it will kill our confidence. We have to play well defensively and we have a good enough squad to score goals."

105

Branislav Ivanovic

CHELSEA V NAPOLI

Stamford Bridge, 14.03.12

Gary Cahill

"Conceding goals is not a nice feeling and on the night [in Napoli] everything went wrong that could have done, so it wasn't a pleasant UEFA Champions League debut and hopefully we can put that right."

John Terry

"Defensively we need to be very solid, but, at the same time, have the players going forward without leaving ourselves too open at the back, so it will be a bit of a mixed bag."

Petr Cech

"We know we can turn it around at home, we have done it for other ties and we need to think we can do it again."

107

Chelsea 4
(Drogba 28, Terry 47, Lampard, pen 75, Ivanovic 104)

Napoli 1
(Inler 54)

(Chelsea win 5-4 on aggregate)

Thrilling comeback lights up the Bridge

What a night! Plenty of talk before the game was about the possibility of another European classic at the Bridge and that is exactly what those watching enjoyed. It needed extra time and a Branislav Ivanovic goal to win it, but the Blues showed bags of character to turn this tie around.

We went ahead on the away goals rule shortly in the second half of normal time, Didier Drogba having scored in the first half and then John Terry adding the second – both goals headers.

But then Napoli, who played their part in the occasion with a very watchable style of football, netted to put them back in front on aggregate, only for Frank Lampard to make the tie level from the penalty spot.

Goals looked possible at either end as the minutes ticked on, but, happily, it was the Blues who did the business to make the quarter-finals and maintain an English challenge in the competition.

Team news

David Luiz, Michael Essien, Juan Mata and Daniel Sturridge returned to the starting line-up for the Blues. David Luiz came in at the expense of Gary Cahill, while Michael Essien and Frank Lampard were in central midfield with Raul Meireles suspended. Juan Mata returned down the middle to support lone striker Didier Drogba, with Daniel Sturridge on the left in place of Salomon Kalou and Ramires operating down the right.

Napoli were unchanged from the first leg.

First Half

Although Chelsea dominated possession at the very start, the game soon settled into the predicted pattern - the home team probing away in front of a well-manned opposition defence but then stretched from time to time by the rapid Napoli attacking play.

Lampard challenged Edinson Cavani hard in the opening seconds but conceded a free-kick on that occasion and Terry sent a header off-target from a Chelsea free-kick, taken by Mata. The first proper effort was by Sturridge, a shot along the deck that the keeper scrambled past the post.

On nine minutes, Napoli for the first time caused trouble for Chelsea, a Hamsik shot deflecting off Terry and needing Cech to quickly shift his weight and save with his legs. Three minutes later the Neapolitan side unleashed just the type of counter-attack that had hurt Chelsea in the first game – Maggio charging into space on the right and firing low to the far post where, on this occasion, Cavani shot wide.

It was worrying times for the Blues and Cech was soon asked to save again, this time from Ezequiel Lavezzi after a very good pass had beaten the offside call.

The coveted early goal for Chelsea hadn't come. Midway through the half Ramires did well to take a Mata pass and spin into the area but the Napoli rearguard was defending well.

It was hard to spot where a Chelsea breakthrough could come from but then Ramires was given the ball out by the left touchline and worked it onto his right foot for a cross. It was perfect for Drogba to head down into the bottom of the Shed End net. We were ahead on the night with 27 minutes played.

We could have been ahead in the tie just a minute later had Hugo Campagnaro not reached the ball just in front of Drogba who looked certain to tap in a Sturridge cross. The Napoli threat remained and Cavani dragged a shot wide after Inler had sent him clear to the frustration of the Napoli fans, but then Sturridge headed not too far wide at the other end.

There was a forced change for the Italian side 10 minutes before the break. Right wing-back Christian Maggio, so lively in the first leg, had not recovered from an early challenge from Ramires whose selection on that wing might have been to use his running against the Italian international. Maggio was replaced by former Liverpool man Andrea Dossena.

Lampard was the first player cautioned, for a 42nd minute foul on Zuniga. It was a stop-start, whistled-filled end to the opening period. In stoppage time David Luiz hammered the ball into the six-yard box and Cannavaro stretched to cut it out, very much running the risk of an own goal in the process.

Second Half

The half was barely a minute old when Cannavaro carelessly headed over his own goal to give Chelsea a corner to tee up a time-honoured combination. Lampard placed his set-piece delivery towards the near-post area where Terry was running towards and the skipper flicked the perfect header over De Sanctis and in.

Napoli had conceded a third of the goals against them that season from headers and it was proving their Achilles heel. Now they had to score.

Cannavaro was booked for a foul on Lampard but the Napoli response was good as Chelsea were soon asked to do plenty of work back in our own area. We conceded an away goal on 54 minutes when Terry initially headed clear a cross but Inler controlled the ball on his chest and sweetly struck it into Cech's net from the edge of the area. Now the Blues needed a goal.

Just prior to Napoli scoring, Di Matteo had been about to bring on Jose Bosingwa, possibly to play on the wing rather than at full-back, but that moment had passed. Instead Torres entered the action with just over an hour played.

The Spaniard was soon foraging hard inside the Napoli area and the ball broke to Ivanovic who smashed a shot that the keeper hurriedly blocked. Then after another Chelsea corner, Drogba battled, spun and unleashed a volley that needed the save of the game from De Sanctis to keep it out of the net.

Dossena was booked on 67 minutes for catching Essien on the thigh before Zuniga came off the flank to force another save from Cech. Some of the Chelsea defending was by now falling into the last-ditch category.

At the other end the corners kept coming, each one bringing hope, and there was a scramble after a sliced Napoli clearance when Drogba had headed on.

The Blues kept the pressure on and Napoli cracked, Dossena clearly handling an

Ivanovic header and on this occasion it was spotted by a UEFA Champions League ref – Felix Brych from Germany pointing to the spot.

Lampard smashed the penalty in to make the scores level on aggregate with 74 minutes played.

The challenges from both sides strengthened. It was a night of blood and thunder, thrills and spills. The Stamford Bridge crowd responded.

With 86 minutes played, David Luiz did well to juggle the ball away from a lurking Cavani and moments later Walter Gargano launched an ambitious effort onto the roof of the Chelsea net. Before the 90 minutes were up, Drogba was wanting a penalty after he and Aronica tangled but this time the ref wasn't interested. Another 30 minutes was to be played.

Extra-time – First Half

The Chelsea threat in the air continued unchecked - Ivanovic this time heading a corner a yard wide, but then Napoli counter-punched with a fierce Hamsik volley that went equally close.

Malouda was the second Chelsea substitute introduced, replacing Mata four minutes into extra time with Bosingwa on three minutes later, a forced change due to a Terry injury. As Ivanovic moved into central defence. Moments before that switch, Cole had been shown a yellow card for fouling Campagnaro.

De Sanctis in the Napoli goal had done well on the night but completely misjudged a long punt forward by Drogba, running underneath it to allow Torres in behind him, but the angle was always against the Spaniard finding the target.

A minute before the interval Chelsea did go ahead – Drogba the craftsman and Ivanovic applying the gleaming finish. In a tight space, the Ivorian wriggled clear enough to cross low and the Serbian turned it in first time from 12 yards out.

Extra-time – Second Half

Ahead on aggregate, now Chelsea could play on the counter-attack and Torres made De Sanctis sprawl to save his long-range shot after Ramires had broken forward.

It was desperate times for the Italian side and Inler and Campagnaro were both booked. One goal for them would turn the tie from a Chelsea win to a Napoli one however, and football doesn't get any more tense than that. The fans inside the Bridge were on the edge of their seats. We could have made it safe with less than a minute left on the clock after Malouda nicked possession high up the pitch and fed Drogba but he volleyed wide. But the four goals proved to be enough. It was time for 'One Step Beyond' as Chelsea took another step forward.

Chelsea (4-4-1-1): Cech; Ivanovic, D Luiz, Terry (c) (Bosingwa 97), Cole; Sturridge (Torres 62); Essien, Lampard, Ramires; Mata (Malouda 94); Drogba. **Unused subs:** Turnbull, Cahill, Mikel, Kalou.
Scorers: Drogba 28, Terry 47, Lampard pen 75, Ivanovic 104. **Booked:** Lampard 42, Cole 97.

Napoli (3-4-2-1): De Sanctis; Campagnaro, Cannavaro (c), Aronica (Vargas 109); Maggio (Dossena 36), Inler, Gargano, Zuniga; Hamsík (Pandev 106), Lavezzi; Cavani.
Unused subs: Rosati, Dzemaili, Fernandez, Britos.
Scorer: Inler 54. **Booked:** Cannavaro 52, Dossena 67, Inler 111, Campagnaro 114.

Referee: Felix Brych (Germany)
Attendance: 37,784

"Everybody was delighted that we put in such a big performance... I have had some great nights [in football] but it will probably go down in the club's history, coming back from a two-goal deficit from the first leg. You saw from the players and how they performed that they showed the passion and that they care about the club and the supporters."

Roberto Di Matteo

"The atmosphere in the stadium was amazing, it made a big difference, we've had some great nights here, but this was one of the best, the semi-final against Liverpool and the Barcelona games were great, but this was fantastic as well."

Didier Drogba

115

"You saw a great spirit, a great energy in the team, the desire, there were people with cramp running at the end and putting their bodies on the line."

Frank Lampard

BENFICA V CHELSEA

Estadio da Luz, 27.03.12

Gary Cahill:

"I am happy with how things are going at the minute. When I first came we played Man United at home and Napoli away, so to play at the standard I expect of myself was hard, but now I'm back to where I should be and need to maintain that.

We have to be confident. Our form of late has been good. We know we have to win the majority of games we have left, and that's our target.

Everyone was saying how bad a season it was, but we're in a quarter-final and a semi-final and are pushing for fourth in the league. It's an important period."

David Luiz:

"I had a good run from the first day I was presented as a Benfica player, we will be mates until the referee starts the match but then their players will become adversaries, and it will be a fight to the end.

We are two good teams against each other and there is pressure for both sets of supporters. Their fans are very passionate, especially at home, but we have the experience to deal with that.

I'm now older and wiser. I have more experience and more responsibility now, everybody knows I love and respect Benfica, but I won't make it easy for them and I want to win."

117

Benfica 0

Chelsea 1
(Kalou 74)

Kalou strike gives Blues advantage

A stark contrast to the Napoli away game as Chelsea matched the home side, defended well and snatched victory thanks to a second-half Salomon Kalou goal.

Benfica had chances, mostly for Oscar Cardoza, and Petr Cech made one excellent save. We also survived a penalty appeal for handball by John Terry but we were rarely clinging on and could have scored more. Juan Mata hit the post and went close again late on in a second half that was far more eventful than the first.

Unlike our previous away games in this UEFA Champions League campaign, on this occasion one goal was enough.

Team news

At right-back, Paulo Ferreira was given his first action of 2012. Branislav Ivanovic was not fit and Jose Bosingwa was on the bench. David Luiz replaced Gary Cahill in the centre.

John Obi Mikel and Raul Meireles were the deeper midfielders. Kalou came in wide on the left and Fernando Torres was preferred to Didier Drogba in attack.

Benfica made one change from their last UEFA Champions League outing, Pablo Aimar replacing Rodrigo as Oscar Cardozo's partner up front.

First Half

Prior to kick-off, David Luiz and Ramires went together to embrace their former manager Jorge Jesus and the Chelsea line-up was not short of players experienced in playing in this stadium, either for or against Benfica. What followed were 45 minutes of football during which the Blues were pretty comfortable, if short of much goal threat ourselves.

There was danger in the fourth minute with the ball bouncing inside the Chelsea six-yard box and Ferreira not able to reach to clear, but it went wide of Cech's far post.

That moment apart, it was a safe opening from the Blues who managed to pressurise their red-shirted opponents into a few errors in midfield. David Luiz on 11 minutes spotted a gap and advanced before hitting a grasscutter wide of the Benfica goal.

On 14 minutes, Ramires clearly showed he had the legs on the Lisbon side's left-back Emerson, sprinting past to help Torres win a corner that keeper Artur punched away limply.

On 17 minutes, Meireles was booked for tripping the flying Gaitan inside the centre-circle. The free-kick was taken quickly, but fortunately Cardozo put a chance wide. It would prove to be their best opportunity of the half.

The next shot was by Torres, taking a David Luiz pass on his chest and then hitting the ball on the turn before it bounced. An ambitious attempt that was off-target.

Benfica midfielder Bruno Cesar was booked for a foul on the advanced Ferreira before there was another chance for Cardozo, a tougher one this time. He was marked by Terry as he headed a cross over. The tricky Aimar had cleverly drawn Mikel and Ramires towards him to make space for the move.

Benfica were pressing high up the pitch and were beginning to take control. Bruno Cesar fancied his chances from distance but struck his shot straight at Cech.

On 38 minutes, Torres did well to surge past his initial marker but when he turned back on his left-foot, his shot flew several yards over.

Two minutes later Kalou teed up Meireles for our first shot on-target. Well-struck and swinging away, Artur had to dive to push it away.

Second Half

No doubt conscious they had to make home advantage count, Benfica came out for the second half with a vigour previously lacking. A throw into the Chelsea area wasn't headed far out by Meireles and Cardozo smacked a shot at the Blues goal that fortuitously hit David Luiz, back on the goal line. A foot either side of him and the Brazilian wouldn't have had time to react.

The Portuguese side kept the pressure on. Bruno Cesar struck another shot straight at Cech.

There was respite when Kalou went on a run and won a free-kick and then shortly after he nipped in front of his marker but headed a Torres cross over.

The placid first half was quickly forgotten as the contest sprang to life. John Terry had been outstanding in dealing with Benfica's crosses and high balls towards Cardozo but he escaped unpunished on the hour when the ball hit his arm away

from his body inside the penalty area, immediately after Cole had acrobatically blocked a shot.

The indignant Benfica would have been even more outraged had Mata scored moments later but the Spaniard struck the woodwork from a tight angle, having beaten the on-rushing goalkeeper to the ball.

On 66 minutes Jardel looked certain to score for Benfica, meeting a diagonal cross at the far post but Cech did brilliantly to push it away. Chelsea broke and it took a foul from Luisao to stop Ramires at the cost of a yellow card.

It was time for a Chelsea change, Lampard a 67th minute substitute for Meireles who, as a former Porto man, received ear-splitting whistling from the home support. Benfica made two changes including introducing former Chelsea midfielder Nemanja Matic.

The Benfica fans were whistling again when Terry just about diverted a dangerous-looking pass with an outstretched foot but despite Cech picking it up, no back pass was the Italian ref's verdict.

Ramires had been among the pick of the Chelsea players and he played his part in the winning goal, taking a painful whack in the process as he played Torres in down the right. The centre-forward again showed his goal-making prowess by picking out Kalou among defenders for a close-range first-time finish.

The Blues could have added a second on the breakaway when substitute Sturrridge charged forward and found Mata but his attempted chip was too high. Before that, Benfica sub Nolito had shot over.

There was still work to do for Chelsea inside stoppage time before the win was secure and, as the ball was hammered threateningly into the danger zone, Cole was once again airborne to send it the right side of the post and ease the tension.

Benfica (4-1-3-2):
Artur; Pereira, Luisão (c), Jardel, Emerson; Garcia (Nolito 81); Gaitán, Witsel, Bruno César (Rodrigo 68); Aimar (Matic 68), Cardozo. **Unused subs:** Eduardo, Oliveira, Miguel Vitor, Saviola. **Booked:** Bruno Cesar 25, Luisão 66, Garcia 74.

Chelsea (4-4-1-1):
Cech; Ferreira (Bosingwa 79), David Luiz, Terry (c), Cole; Ramires, Meireles (Lampard 67), Mikel, Kalou (Sturrridge 82); Mata; Torres. **Unused subs:** Turnbull, Cahill, Essien, Drogba. **Scorer:** Kalou 74. **Booked:** Meireles 17.

Referee: Paolo Tagliavento (Italy)
Attendance: 60,830

"I always felt we looked solid defensively, well organised and I always fancied us to score a goal. We're pleased we are in a different position going into the next leg. We had a mountain to climb against Napoli, this will be as well but it will be a bit smaller because we had a good result here. We'll see what we can do, but it's a dangerous result if we think we've already qualified, we cannot think we're through yet. We've put ourselves in a good position, yes, but it's not a result you can rely on for the home game."

Roberto Di Matteo

"Every day I do my work and try to be in the best condition if the manager wants me. This game he chose me and I tried to give my best. Another day I could do even better but in physical terms I knew that I couldn't make crazy runs so I needed to play with more intelligence."

Paulo Ferreira

"When we play as a team it is very difficult to beat us. It was a great result winning away and not conceding a goal and if you want to go far in the UEFA Champions League you have to play as a team, and on the night we showed we are a great team. Now our worst enemy can be ourselves, thinking that we have done the most difficult job."

Salomon Kalou

125

CHELSEA V BENFICA

Stamford Bridge, 04.04.12

Ramires:

"It will certainly be a difficult game. We have an important advantage from the first game, obviously, but we have 90 tough minutes in front of us and we are going to face a serious challenge."

John Mikel Obi:

"I come in every day and try to enjoy what I do, enjoy my work and have a smile on my face. If that's working it's good, football is a job I love doing and one I want to do full of happiness. Playing makes me feel like that and I'm pleased that the coach has confidence in me.

The away goal last week could be important for us, it was very important we got that result out in Portugal because now we are in the driving seat but the job is not yet done.

For me it's only 40 per cent done, they will come here and give us a game, they won't sit back, so we have to keep playing and try to stop them doing the same. Hopefully that will be enough to give us the win we want to go through to the semi-finals."

127

Chelsea 2
(Lampard, pen 20, Meireles 90+2)

Benfica 1
(Garcia 84)

Blues through after a nervous night

It took a late Raul Meireles goal to settle Chelsea nerves after a game drifting towards a comfortable, if unspectacular, home win was brought back to life by an 84th minute Benfica goal.

It was a much stronger performance by the Lisbon club than had been witnessed on their home turf but after Frank Lampard had put his side ahead from the penalty spot and the visitors had been reduced to 10 men by a sending off for Maxi Pereira, Chelsea were well on course for the semi-finals.

However, Benfica always carried a threat and Javi Garcia made it 1-1.

With the scores still level, the Portuguese outfit committed men forward in stoppage time, searching for the goal that would have sent them into the semi-final, but it was Chelsea who scored a late winner.

Team news

129

Ramires, such a problem to Benfica left-back Emerson in the first leg, played again on the right of midfield. Scorer in Portugal Salomon Kalou was on the other flank and Fernando Torres continued in attack. Didier Drogba was fit enough to return to the bench, while David Luiz was able to start, despite having to come off in the preceding league game.

In contrast, Benfica were missing both centre-backs from the first leg, captain ❯

Luisão and Jardel, so Emerson moved across to the middle and Spanish World Cup winner Joan Capdevila came in on the left of their defence. Former Chelsea man Nemanja Matic was handed a start in midfield.

First Half

Chelsea had to defend almost non-stop for the first four minutes as Benfica, attacking the Shed End containing their fans, started with a high tempo. There were important block tackles from Frank Lampard and John Terry on the edge of our area before we eventually took the ball inside the opposition half.

The Blues won our first corner on seven minutes, flicked on to David Luiz in space who rifled a shot goalwards, blocked well by the leg of Capdevila.

We threatened to cut through the Portuguese side on the break soon after but Mata got his angles wrong in attempting to find Torres ahead of him. Mata had the ball in the net seconds later, but had run offside in the move.

The Slovenian ref wasn't slow to blow for physical contact and on 18 minutes he produced a yellow card for the first time. David Luiz had anticipated well, nipping between Oscar Cardozo and the ball and receiving a kick on the ankle from the Benfica striker as a reward.

A minute later the ref was reaching for his card again, this time in the aftermath of awarding Chelsea a penalty. Cole had just taken down a lofted ball forward when he was bundled to the floor by stand-in centre-back Garcia. Bruno Cesar and Maxi Pereira were booked.

The keeper went the correct way with his dive but Lampard found the bottom corner with his spot kick for his 22nd UEFA Champions League goal. Chelsea were 2-0 up on aggregate with 20 minutes of the second leg played.

Five minutes later, there was more vulnerability at the back from Benfica when everyone missed a long punt from Cech. Torres ran clear and although forced wide, still managed to deliver a cross that could have led to a goal.

Aimar made it three Benfica bookings for dissent and four overall before his side came close to a goal with a free-kick routine. Initially played out wide, it was eventually nodded down to Carodozo who beat Cech with his shot but Terry blocked on the line and Ivanovic cleared.

Ivanovic was the first Chelsea name in the book on 37 minutes for a trip on Gaitan. The Benfica free-kick that followed was played straight into the Chelsea wall.

The cards kept coming on this stop-start evening and when Pereira slid his studs into Mikel's shin, he saw his second yellow and had to walk early down the tunnel.

Ramires was cautioned for a late tackle on Bruno Cesar who was now right-back. Prior to that the Brazilian fired a low ball across the area but just out of the reach of Torres and Kalou.

Second Half

Three minutes after the restart, Cech needed to produce his best save of the game after Cardozo swung a leg at a bouncing ball and sent it towards the top corner. Our keeper dived, extended one of those long arms and sent the ball over.

A minute later and up the other end, Ramires missed the chance for a Chelsea second after Kalou had deceived Bruno Cesar at the far post and shot for the opposite corner. His Brazilian team-mate slid in and made contact but the player rather than the ball ended up in the net.

Torres turned sharply inside the area and looked to have placed his shot inside the post but it was deflected just wide and Kalou headed a Mata cross wide. Chelsea had started the second half much better than the first.

A second goal looked like it was coming but Artur saved acrobatically from Mata before Benfica made a surprising substitution, taking off Cardozo and bringing on Oliveira. Chelsea made a sub too, replacing Terry with Cahill. The skipper went straight down the tunnel for treatment.

Chelsea's grip on the half loosened a little when Ivanovic misdirected a header and another substitute, Djalo, had a goal-bound shot deflected wide by Cahill. Kalou, who was seeing plenty of ball on the left, could have scored but the keeper managed to save his effort. Against a side with reduced numbers and inexperience in the heart of their defence, the missed chances were a source of frustration for Blues fans.

Mata was next to shoot wide, having been teed-up by a skilful Kalou pass but although there was more of a goal threat about Chelsea this half, we were looking less secure at the back. Djalo headed a cross just over Cech's crossbar.

On 74 minutes, MIkel spread the play out to Cole who crossed low. Kalou controlled it, spun but shot wide again.

The card count was much reduced in the second half and Cole and David Luiz ⊘

managed to avoid bookings that would have ruled them out of the first game against Barcelona, but Mikel did pick up a caution for tripping Matic.

On 84 minutes came the Benfica goal. Cech had only just saved well to prevent Djalo heading in but from the corner that followed, Garcia ran unmarked to flick home with his head.

Happily, inside the four minutes of stoppage time that were played, substitute Meireles, was able to charge from his own half against a depleted Benfica backline, stretched even further by a supporting run from Ramires. The Portuguese international, once again much booed by the Benfica fans, smashed the ball into the net and Chelsea were through.

A repeat of the 2009 UEFA Champions League semi-final awaited, although this time Barcelona would visit us first.

Chelsea (4-2-3-1):
Cech; Ivanovic, David Luiz, Terry (c) (Cahill 59), Cole; Mikel, Lampard; Ramires, Mata (Meireles 79), Kalou; Torres (Drogba 88) **Unused subs:** Turnbull, Ferreira, Essien, Sturridge. **Scorers:** Lampard pen 20, Meireles 90+2. **Booked:** Ivanovic 37, Ramires 43, Mikel 78.

Benfica (4-1-3-2):
Artur; Pereira (c), Garcia, Emerson, Capdevila; Matic; Bruno César (Rodrigo 72), Witsel, Gaitán (Djalo 61); Cardozo (Oliveira 56), Aimar **Unused subs:** Eduardo, Almeida, Nolito, Saviola. **Scorer:** Garcia 84. **Booked:** Cardozo 18, Bruno Cesar 19, Pereira 19, Aimar 27. **Sent off:** Pereira 39 (2 yellows).

Referee: Domir Skomina (Slovenia)
Attendance: 37,264

"Even though 1-0 away was a great result it leaves you with a bit of conundrum in terms of how to approach the game. We were sitting on a result so you don't want to go too gung-ho, but we created enough chances in the second half to wrap it up without dominating the game, and when you see those chances keep going past the post, you know if they get their goal it's going to give you a dodgy few minutes."

Frank Lampard

"We are in the semi-finals and it is a gift for us to be there. Barcelona have most of the best players in the world but we are Chelsea and we will fight. Are they beatable? In football nothing is impossible. Of course, it will be difficult. They can play just as well away as they can at home but we shall see. We are a side with more confidence now. That is the reason for our recent results."

Juan Mata

"We expected it was going to be a hard game and it exactly proved to be that. We made it more difficult for ourselves by not scoring a goal in the second half with all those chances, and that kept Benfica alive. We knew they were a good side and we were happy for a 1-0 lead but we knew the game wasn't over. I said at half time that we needed that second goal to kill the game off. Every time you don't do that you know it is going to be hard work until the ref blows the whistle."

Roberto Di Matteo

135

CHELSEA V BARCELONA

Stamford Bridge, 18.04.12

Didier Drogba:

"It is 50-50, even if Barcelona are set to be the best team in the world and they have the best player in the world. It is two games, anything can happen."

Frank Lampard:

"It is a huge occasion to play a semi-final and we are playing against the top team in world football recently. What better challenge to take on as a team. The players and the club remain as determined as ever to win the UEFA Champions League."

Roberto Di Matteo:

137

"They don't like to play against us, results in the past have shown that. The way we play is difficult for them to play against. We respect each other, but there will be two teams playing against each other and we will try to cause them problems."

Chelsea 1
(Drogba 45+2)

Barcelona 0

Top Drog gives magnificent Blues crucial lead

A pulsating encounter at Stamford Bridge meant the Blues headed to Spain with a slender 1-0 advantage after Didier Drogba's strike late in the first half proved the difference on the night.

It was a remarkable performance by the Blues, carrying out Roberto Di Matteo's instructions to a tee, and while we lived dangerously at times, it was a result our bravery merited in the end.

Alexis Sanchez and Cesc Fabregas had gone close to opening the scoring for the visitors in the first half, while after the break Petr Cech saved well from Carlos Puyol. Right at the death, Pedro was denied by the post, but we held on for a famous win.

Ultimately, it was a result which stood us in good stead for the return leg.

Team news

Following the impressive 5-1 drubbing of Tottenham in the FA Cup semi-final, Roberto Di Matteo made only two changes to the side which started the game at Wembley.

With David Luiz unavailable after aggravating his hamstring at the weekend, Gary Cahill made his first start in the UEFA Champions League since the away leg in Napoli, while there was also a start for Raul Meireles, who came in for Salomon Kalou, with Frank Lampard playing further forward. Drogba, so often the man for the big occasion, started up front for the Blues.

For Barcelona, Puyol was passed fit and captained the side in central defence alongside Javier Mascherano, who was preferred to Gerard Pique.

First Half

Although the visitors enjoyed plenty of possession in the opening stages, Chelsea looked to utilise the threat of Drogba on the break, and it almost paid dividends on two separate occasions, only for the Catalan defence to come out on top both times.

The Spanish side's ability to open teams up at will was apparent, however, when Andres Iniesta played a ball over the top of the Blues' back-four and Alexis Sanchez raced on to it before lifting his strike beyond Cech, only to see it bounce back off the bar.

It was a frenetic opening to the game, and while Drogba was penalised for a tackle on Sergio Busquets, the home crowd quickly became aggrieved as decision after decision went Barcelona's way.

Lionel Messi had been a peripheral figure for the opening 10 minutes, but a trademark run saw the Argentinian tee up Iniesta whose shot was parried by Cech. The rebound fell directly into the path of Cesc Fabregas, but as the former Arsenal man looked destined to break the deadlock, he scuffed his strike and allowed Chelsea to clear.

The ability of Pep Guardiola's side to retain possession before finding a killer pass was beginning to tell, and Cech had to be alert twice in quick succession to prevent Messi from opening the scoring, while Iniesta felt he was pulled down in the penalty area by Cahill, one of the few decisions that went our way early on.

Xavi, so often the man who makes the holders of the trophy tick, was dictating the pace of the game, with one particular pass seeking out Daniel Alves requiring a last-ditch clearance from Ashley Cole.

Three minutes before the break, Mikel lost out to Messi on the halfway line, and as the forward broke at speed, he slipped in the advancing Fabregas to his left who cleverly lifted the ball beyond Cech, but as the away fans began to celebrate, Cole, once again, made a wonderful clearance off the line to keep Barca at bay.

Having defended magnificently, the Blues took the lead in added time of the first half. Lampard sprayed it out wide to Ramires, and as the Brazilian fizzed a cross to the back post, Drogba was on hand to force his strike beyond Valdes to give us a priceless advantage, his fifth goal in this season's tournament. Stamford Bridge went wild.

Second Half

Barcelona, clearly stung by that late first-half strike by Drogba, came out for the second half on the front foot, and Cech was forced into an impressive early save from a curling Adriano effort, while Cahill made a fantastic block from a Messi strike.

Minutes later Sanchez fired wide after exchanging passes with Messi, before Alves blazed high over the bar from an Iniesta cross.

It was Cahill again who brought a roaming Messi run to a halt as the Argentine took on three Blues defenders, and our January acquisition was enjoying one of his most impressive games in a Blue shirt.

As the game wore on, Messi's influence on proceedings began to increase, and another marauding run required an expertly timed block from John Terry.

Guardiola, sensing an opening, made the first change of the evening, replacing Sanchez with Pedro in a straight swap, while both Ramires and the Barcelona substitute found themselves booked in the space of a couple of minutes for late, albeit fairly innocuous, challenges.

Salomon Kalou was introduced to the action with just under 20 minutes remaining, replacing Juan Mata as Di Matteo sensed the necessity for fresh legs.

Fabregas made way for Thiago with 10 minutes left to play, but it was backs to the walls for the Blues as we came under an inevitable flurry of pressure from the European champions.

Much like the first 45 minutes, clear-cut opportunities were few, not that the home fans were bothered, as they sung their hearts out, willing their team on.

Cech made a stunning save with five minutes left on the clock, as Puyol flicked on a teasing Messi free-kick which was delivered at pace, making the stop all the more special.

Di Matteo replaced Ramires with Bosingwa in an attempt to shore things up in the closing stages, while Drogba became the second Chelsea player to have his name taken by Felix Brych.

Barcelona looked to have stolen a late equaliser in the dying seconds when Pedro's effort beat Cech, only to bounce back off the foot of the post, while Busquets could only smash the rebound high up into the Shed End.

It was to be the last chance of the game and we took a precious, hard-won advantage into the second leg.

Chelsea (4-5-1):
Cech; Ivanovic, Cahill, Terry (c), Cole; Mata (Kalou 73), Lampard, Mikel, Meireles, Ramires (Bosingwa 87); Drogba. **Unused subs:** Turnbull, Essien, Malouda, Torres, Sturridge.
Scorer: Drogba 45+2. **Booked:** Ramires 68, Drogba 85.

Barcelona (4-3-3):
Valdes; Alves, Puyol (c), Mascherano, Adriano; Xavi (Cuenca 86), Busquets, Iniesta; Sanchez (Pedro Rodriguez 66), Messi, Fabregas (Thiago 78).
Unused subs: Pinto, Pique, Bartra, Keita. **Booked:** Pedro 70, Busquets 75.

Referee: Felix Brych (Germany)
Attendance: 38,039

"We had to defend, because Barcelona kept a lot of the ball, and take advantage of our chances to score – and we did it. We achieved a good result for us. We had two or three chances to score and 1-0 is a good result."

Juan Mata

"Our midfielders had to work really hard and Didier up front on his own as well. It was a great, tireless performance from everyone."

John Terry

145

"I think we deserved it because of the way we kept our focus throughout the 90 minutes, we got the reward of a good result."

Petr Cech

BARCELONA V CHELSEA

Camp Nou, 24.04.12

Petr Cech:

"I think it will be the same type of game as the first leg, and I hope we can score again. A goal for us is going to make a big difference in terms of the whole game."

Ramires:

"It is about our focus and concentration, and the desire of our players. Of course it is difficult but we know it is not impossible. We have to respect Barcelona and know how strong they are, but we are very strong too. If we have the same, or even more desire than we had at Stamford Bridge, everything is possible for us."

Roberto Di Matteo:

147

"Ultimately Barcelona will create chances against any team and we will have to try to score a goal, but we will also try to limit the chances they create against us.

It is too difficult to play for a goalless draw. To score would give us a greater advantage but we all know how difficult it is going to be."

Barcelona 2
(Busquets 34, Iniesta 43)

Chelsea 2
(Ramires 45+1, Torres 90+1)

(Chelsea win 3-2 on aggregate)

Destination Munich as heroes overcome the odds

There cannot have been many nights more dramatic or heroic in the history of Chelsea Football Club.

Having gone 2-0 behind on the night and one man down in the first half, we scored in stoppage time at the end of each half to book a date in Munich for our second UEFA Champions League Final.

Ramires was the first Chelsea scorer with a brilliant goal before Lionel Messi wasted the chance to put his side 3-1 ahead when he missed a penalty.

With the pressure on, substitute Fernando Torres scored a late goal on the counter-attack from his own half. The only disappointment on a joyous night was that Ramires, Branislav Ivanovic and Raul Meireles were all booked and so joined John Terry – who had been sent off in the first half – in missing the final.

Team news

149

Didier Drogba was passed fit so Roberto Di Matteo named the same side as the first leg. Barcelona did change, however, bringing in Gerard Pique and going to three at the back. Both full-backs at the Bridge were on the bench with Issac Cuenca coming in and playing wide on the right with Cesc Fabregas on the left. The formation was the same as deployed in Camp Nou in the previous round against AC Milan.

First Half

Chelsea showed good attacking intent from the whistle as Ashley Cole's incisive pass breached the Barça penalty area within 18 seconds but Valdes collected just ahead of the on-rushing Ramires.

The Blues were awarded the first free-kick of the game for a foul on Mata on halfway.

But then Barcelona attacked and Messi had his first chance with two minutes played. He put it into the side-netting from inside the area.

The pressure stayed on for almost the whole of the rest of the half and there was a problem for the Blues on six minutes when the ball was played behind Cahill to Sanchez. In recovering, the big Chelsea defender slipped and almost did the splits. He needed treatment but after a spell off the pitch, initially continued.

Iniesta lobbed a ball into the six-yard box that Cole booted clear before finally, on 11 minutes, Cahill had to limp off dejectedly to be replaced by Bosingwa. Ivanovic went into central defence.

It wasn't only Chelsea players in the wars. On 17 minutes Drogba chased a Cech kick that bounced high up field and in clearing it, Valdes collided with Pique. Both needed treatment and the Barcelona central defender looked in some distress, but given recovery time he was back in action.

On 19 minutes it was Cech's time to turn hero. A trademark exchange of passes by the home team cut through the Chelsea defence, Fabregas backheeling into the path of Messi, but with the Camp Nou crowd drawing breath to celebrate, our keeper's leg extended and made the save.

There was a rare Chelsea attempt from Drogba at the midway point of the half but on the swivel and from distance, he shot well over.

He was much closer to the target two minutes later after muscling past Pique but lacking support, he took on Valdes from a very narrow angle and could only ripple the sidenetting.

That was the end of Pique's game. The previous Chelsea attack had convinced Pep Guardiola the player was still suffering from his bang on the head and he brought on Dani Alves. They didn't change their shape with the diminutive substitute deployed as one of the back three.

Referee Cüneyt Çakir had given Chelsea no cause for complaint with his decisions so far but he did make Mikel his first booking, the midfielder catching Sanchez with an outstretched leg inside the Barça half.

Three minutes later the home team took the lead. The move was similar to many during the half but for once Chelsea found themselves outnumbered as the ball was played wide to the left after Drogba had headed away a corner. Cuenca was out there and he squared to Busquets who side-footed in from six yards out.

Any chance for consolidation after that set-back for Roberto Di Matteo's men was blown out the water just two minutes later with the straight red card for Terry. Now Bosingwa would have to play more centrally and Ramires' defensive responsibilities increased.

A tough task had just become immensely harder and Barcelona went further ahead three minutes before the interval. Meireles conceded possession and Messi was able to slip the ball forward to Iniesta who had run away behind Ramires. The finish was low to Cech's left and for the first time in the tie Chelsea were behind on aggregate. Ramires was booked for arguing about no offside flag and would miss the final as well as Terry, should the Blues find a way back from this.

We certainly made a good start in that quest. Despite his increased defensive duties, and the psychological blow of that yellow card, Ramires turned the tie back in our favour with a moment of sublime impudence and sheer brilliance.

With just a minute of stoppage time left to play we won the ball and Ramires drove forward into the Barça half. Lampard slotted the perfect ball through to the Brazilian. There was no way the Barça defence was going to catch him and his chip over Valdes was as exquisite as it was essential to restore belief before the break. With the score 2-2 on aggregate, it was Chelsea heading to the final as it stood.

Second Half

Barcelona made an alteration to the way they lined up with Alves now wide on the right and Cuenca switching wings.

Just three minutes into the half the Blues looked certain to go behind in the tie when Drogba tripped Fabregas inside the area but Messi fired the penalty on to the crossbar. The Argentinian's search for his first goal against Chelsea went on.

If that was good news, Ivanovic's booking in the aftermath of the penalty award wasn't. He joined Terry and Ramires in earning a suspension. Iniesta was the first Barça player booked, for a trip on Drogba.

Di Matteo decided on fresh legs just before the hour, replacing Mata with Kalou, ◉

and a minute later Cech was booked for taking too long over a goal-kick.

It was all Barcelona pressure and Cech saved from Cuenca. On 63 minutes Chelsea broke out of our shackles and Drogba won a corner. Played in by Lampard, Ivanovic got to it first but couldn't send it on target.

The cards kept coming, Messi for a foul on Lampard, who then upended Fabregas. And still Chelsea hung on to the away-goals lead as, heroically, shot after shot and pass after pass were blocked.

In the 79th minute Torres came on for Drogba who had worked tirelessly up front. He had also played his part, as ever, in clearing opposition corners.

Barcelona did have the ball in the net on 80 minutes through Sanchez but Alves, who supplied the cross, was offside. Then Messi shot on-target and it was turned onto the post by the fingertips of Cech.

We were inside the final 10 minutes and now every Barça mistake was drawing a frustrated reaction from the crowd. When Chelsea won the ball, we by and large cleared it into the open spaces up the field.

With 88 minutes of the game played, Meireles picked up a booking, meaning he would also be suspended for the final. Cech then pushed a Mascherano shot round the post and we were into stoppage time.

It was time for the most dramatic of endings. Barcelona were so committed forward that when the ball was cleared up field by Cole, Torres was in his half with no-one between him and Valdes. He took the ball on and went past the keeper before slotting in, as he had done so many times in the past against this opposition – and it was good night Barcelona as we headed for Munich.

Chelsea (4-5-1):
Cech; Ivanovic, Cahill (Bosingwa 12), Terry (c), Cole; Mata (Kalou 57), Lampard, Mikel, Meireles, Ramires; Drogba (Torres 79). **Unused subs:** Turnbull, Essien, Malouda, Sturridge. **Scorers:** Ramires 45+1, Torres 90+1. **Booked:** Mikel 31, Ramires 44, Ivanovic 47, Cech 58, Lampard 71, Meireles 88. **Sent-off:** Terry 36.

Barcelona (3-1-4-2):
Valdes; Mascherano, Pique (Alves 25), Puyol (c); Busquets; Cuenca (Tello 67), Xavi, Fabregas (Kieta 73), Iniesta; Sanchez, Messi. **Unused subs:** Busquets 34, Iniesta 43. **Scorers:** Busquets 34, Iniesta 43. **Booked:** Iniesta 49, Messi 70.

Referee: Cüneyt Çakir (Turkey)
Attendance: 95,845.

"It was a magnificent night for everyone involved with the club; the players, the staff, the fans who have come out here, the fans at home. There's no coincidence in what Robbie's done, he's got players playing, he's created an atmosphere and the camp's very happy. Results don't lie and I can't speak highly enough of him."

Frank Lampard

"It was an incredible game. There were so many events. I am very happy but most of all pleased for the players because they deserve this. They have had a difficult season and they seem to be able to do something special when they need to. This seems to be the DNA of these players. We seem to find some reserves from somewhere. It is just incredible."

155

Roberto Di Matteo

Bayern Munich 1
(Muller 82)

Chelsea 1
(Drogba 87)

(Chelsea win 4-3 on penalties after extra-time)

Summary

We thought we had seen it all during an extraordinary UEFA Champions League campaign. On a night of immense tension and suspense in Munich, there was plenty more drama to come with a glorious, joyous finish.

Showing the resilience that had taken us all the way to the final, Didier Drogba netted his ninth goal in nine cup finals with two minutes left to play to equalise Thomas Muller's header.

Petr Cech then saved an Arjen Robben penalty, given away by Drogba in extra-time, so 10 more spot-kicks had to be taken to determine the destiny of the UEFA Champions League trophy.

It didn't start well as Juan Mata failed with Chelsea's first but Cech saved one and Bastian Schweinsteiger struck the woodwork before that man Drogba stepped up to win the competition for the first time for a London club, with the satisfaction that it had been achieved in our opponents' stadium and came with the added prize of qualification for next season's UEFA Champions League.

Team news

Roberto Di Matteo decided upon Ryan Bertrand in front of Ashley Cole on the flank that Arjen Robben and Philipp Lahm attack down for Bayern. David Luiz and Gary Cahill were fit to start with Jose Bosingwa completing the defence. Frank Lampard and John Mikel Obi were the deeper midfielders with Juan Mata in front of them, Salomon Kalou on the right and Didier Drogba leading the attack. Bayern replaced their two suspended defenders with Diego Contento and Anatoliy Tymoshchuk, the latter deployed at centre-back. Thomas Muller came into midfield.

First Half

The pre-match proceedings were loud and colourful with both sets of fans playing their part. The Blues support were in fine voice and the 'Pride of London' flag travelled with them.

Then it was time for kick-off, Chelsea attacking towards the German side's supporters. Lampard tackled Robben and then Cole went in hard on Kroos to give away a free-kick in the opening seconds.

Inside two minutes Schweinsteiger was booked for a clear handball as Mikel tried to play out from the back and find Lampard.

Bayern advanced on four minutes and Schweinsteiger shot but Cahill stretched out a long leg and deflected it for a corner.

Chelsea's first attack came with six minutes played, a few passes leading to a Drogba cross that was overhit. Chelsea kept the pressure on but then Robben broke threateningly, only to sky his shot badly.

Bayern were dominating possession but without the feeling they were about to break through the Chelsea defence. Gomez, stretching over the top of David Luiz, headed a cross over.

On 17 minutes Robben met a Kroos corner with a half-volley but it was deflected for another corner which led to the scariest moment yet when Gomez tricked Cahill. Lampard couldn't get the ball out of the six-yard box and Bosingwa sliced his clearance behind him but into a safe zone.

Cech then had to be at his best to turn wide a Robben shot after the former Blue wriggled past Bosingwa.

Just before the half-hour, David Luiz put an arm across the front of Muller and fouled him, although Robben's free-kick was a long way off clearing the Chelsea defensive wall. The former Chelsea man did not have a good night.

Two minutes later we briefly found space and Bertrand, supplied by Mata, took on Lahm but the German international stood firm and made the necessary tackle.

On 32 minutes, Cahill was found upfield by Kalou and drew a foul out of Boateng. It was just outside the area, a bit to the right and made for the left foot of Mata, but the Spaniard shot several yards over the bar.

Three minutes later Bayern missed their best chance yet, Muller found unmarked near the penalty spot by Contento but he volleyed wide. Wayward shooting by the men in red continued as one of the themes of the night.

Suddenly the ball was up the other end and Drogba was battling with the Bayern central defence, but he was crowded out.

Seeing Chelsea on the offensive seemed to inspire the players and Bertrand picked out Drogba who in turn played the ball out wide to an unmarked Kalou. The shot was low and hard and forced the first save out of Neuer.

However, as we pressed, Bayern became more of a counter-attacking threat and there was much relief when Gomez shot well over when presented with a golden chance.

Second Half

The first-half stats had shown 60 per cent possession to Bayern with eight corners to our nil and 13 attempts on goal to just two from the team from London. The options were to hope for a smash and grab or find some way of taking the game to a side with an unfamiliar defence.

Ribery attacked and shot after Chelsea lost the ball within a minute of the restart but David Luiz blocked it inside the six-yard box. The Brazilian then got his positioning wrong to let Robben past but Cole saved the day initially and then David Luiz was able to head a shot to safety.

Drogba didn't waste the opportunity to attempt a spectacular effort on the turn from distance on 50 minutes but didn't trouble Neuer.

Bayern had the ball in the net soon after but Ribery had lashed it in from an offside position. It was a sign, though, that they were finding increasing space around our penalty area and the defiant Cole needed to be razor-sharp to block Robben's attempt after Gomez had shown good control.

The game entered the final half-hour with Bayern continuing to drag shots wide. Chelsea's attacking potential was diminished by diligent crowding of Mata when he was on the ball.

Cole again threw himself in the way of a shot, this time from Kroos before, on 71 minutes, Chelsea broke our shackles and Kalou wasn't too far away at all from

making something of a Bosingwa cross. Then Drogba got away down the left and nearly picked out Mata right in front of goal but Bayern cleared for a corner.

Drogba could have made them pay soon after but didn't catch a shot properly. Were Bayern starting to fear the sucker punch?

Malouda had by now come on for Bertrand who seemed to indicate a problem to the bench a minute earlier. Ribery, inside the Chelsea area on the right, shot and it deflected up and dropped worryingly but Cech stretched back to make sure the ball went over the bar. Muller then waited for the ball to fall on his right-foot after an attack started by Schweinsteiger but his shot was a long way wide.

Cole became Chelsea's first booking for a foul on Muller who, soon after, finally found the breakthrough.

Kroos was allowed to cross towards the far post unchallenged and Muller headed down, able to beat Cech with a ball that bounced up above the Chelsea keeper and in off the underside of the bar. There were 82 minutes played.

Torres came on for Kalou, David Luiz was booked, and it was hard to see any way back into this game for Di Matteo's men. Almost inevitably, one man from the Ivory Coast had other ideas.

Never underestimate Didier Drogba in a cup final. Mata sent a corner over towards the near post and the Ivorian thundered a header through the tiny gap between Neuer and his crossbar.

He could have even won it in stoppage time after Bayern gave away a free-kick in a very promising position, but the shot was too high.

Extra-time – First Period

It was a bright start by the Blues but then with three minutes gone, Drogba caught the heel of Ribery and gave away a penalty. It fell to Robben to try to beat his friend Cech but the pressure told, as it had done on Lionel Messi in the semi-final, and the Chelsea keeper was able to save low down to his left as Robben couldn't find the corner. Ribery didn't recover from the foul by Drogba and was replaced by Ivica Olic.

Extra-time – Second Period

Bayern could have retaken the lead two minutes in when Olic was found all alone at the far post and sprayed the ball across to Van Buyten, but the substitute hadn't reacted quickly enough to tap into the gaping net.

Chelsea survived another goalmouth scramble after which Cahill, who played a mighty game, felt the effect of those weeks out, needing treatment for cramp.

Torres was booked for dissent after giving away a foul as he sought a last-minute winner but it was to be the gut-wrenching experience of a shoot-out once again.

Penalty Shoot-out

At the Bayern Munich end of the stadium, Cech faced the first one from Lahm and got a hand to it but couldn't keep it out.

Mata then had his saved by Neuer. Gomez found the bottom corner to make it 2-0 to Bayern but David Luiz scored his powerfully and it was 2-1.

The Bayern keeper took the next one, and beat Cech low to the left so it was 3-1 to the Germans. Lampard roofed his to bring the score back to 3-2 before Olic had his saved by the outstretched arm of Cech and Cole drew the scores level at 3-3 with a crisp strike.

Schweinsteiger was next up and the pressure told as he hit the post, Cech getting fingers to it. So it was there for Drogba to win it and the Ivorian kept his composure to roll the ball home as scenes of unbridled joy erupted in the Chelsea ranks.

Bayern Munich (4-2-3-1): Neuer; Lahm (c), Tymoshchuk, Boateng, Contento; Schweinsteiger, Kroos; Robben, T Muller (Van Buyten 85), Ribéry (Olic 96); Gomez.
Unused subs: Butt, Rafinha, Usami, Pranjic, Petersen.
Goals: Muller 82.
Shoot-out Penalties: Lahm, Gomez, Neuer. **Booked:** Schweinsteiger 1.

Chelsea (4-2-3-1): Cech; Bosingwa, Cahill, David Luiz, Cole; Mikel, Lampard (c); Kalou (Torres 83), Mata, Bertrand (Malouda 73); Drogba.
Unused subs: Turnbull, Ferreira, Essien, Romeu, Sturridge.
Goals: Drogba 87.
Shoot-out Penalties: David Luiz, Lampard, Cole, Drogba. **Booked:** Cole 80, David Luiz 85, Drogba 93, Torres 119.

Referee: Pedro Proença (Portugal)
Attendance: 62,500

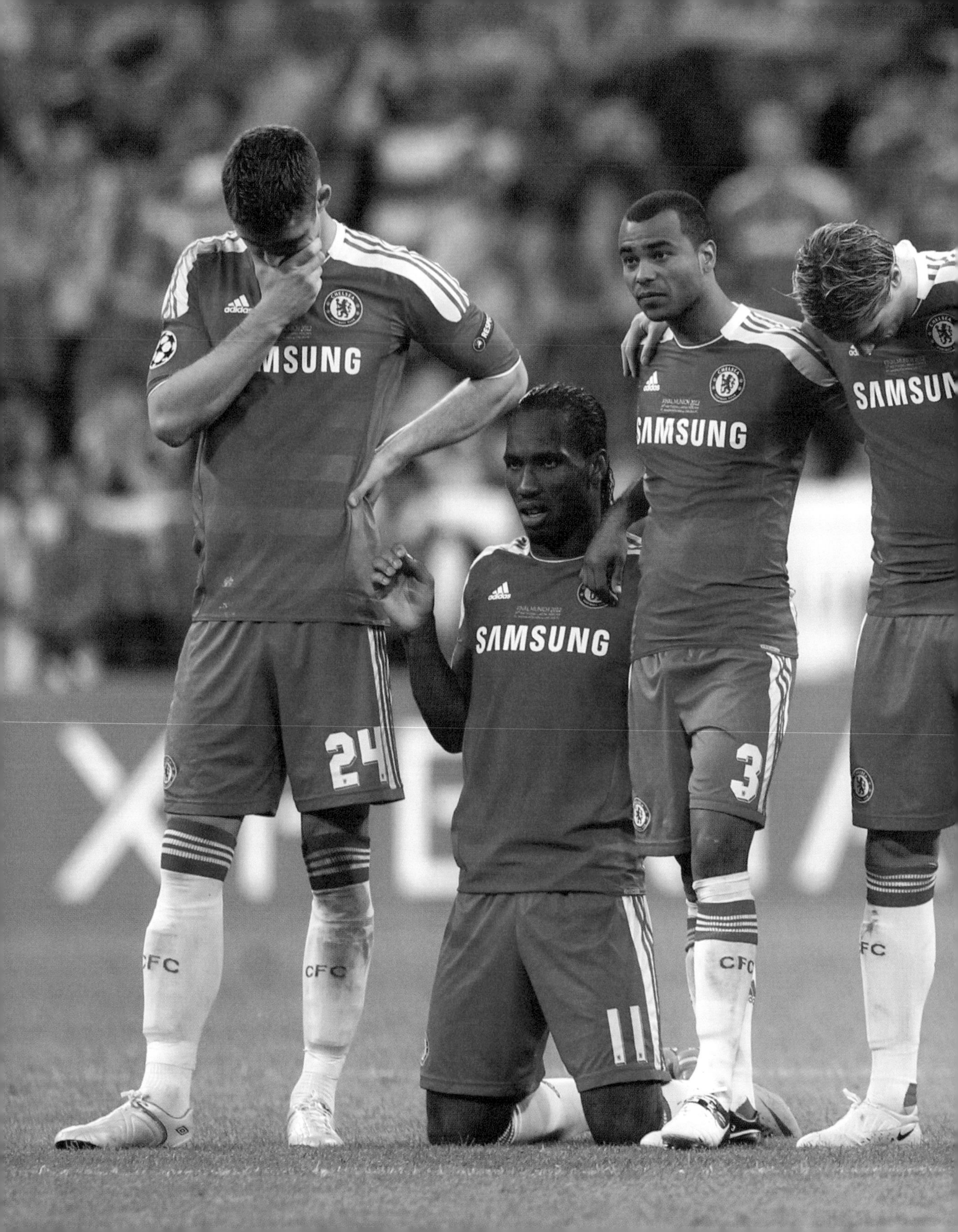
SAMSUNG
SAMSUNG
SAMSUNG
SAMSUNG

Drogba ends night of drama

First blood to Bayern Munich, as skipper Philipp Lahm guesses right at the coin toss and the penalty shoot-out will take place at the end of the stadium housing the home supporters. The full-back then steps up to take the first kick and places his effort to the left of Petr Cech, who gets fingertips to the ball but can't prevent it finding the net.

Bayern Munich 1-0 Chelsea

Juan Mata is Chelsea's first penalty taker but Manuel Neuer dives to his left to palm away the Spaniard's attempt.

Bayern Munich 1-0 Chelsea

He spurned several good chances during his 120 minutes on the pitch, so how will Mario Gomez fare when he makes the long walk from the centre circle to take aim at Cech's goal? Very well, as it happens – a low, crisp strike gives the Blues No.1 no chance.

Bayern Munich 2-0 Chelsea

171

An incredible performance by David Luiz deserves to end with a successful penalty – and the Brazilian banishes the memory of his missed spot-kick against Genk in the group phase with an unstoppable shot into the roof of the net after an unusually long run-up.

Bayern Munich 2-1 Chelsea

There is confusion in the Fussball Arena Munchen, as no Bayern player makes the long walk from the halfway line to take their third penalty. Instead, it's goalkeeper Neuer who is entrusted with beating his opposite number. Cech goes the right way for the third time, but once again the strike is too good.

Bayern Munich 3-1 Chelsea

When it comes to high-pressure situations, Frank Lampard is a man you want to see stepping up to the plate. The Blues' stand-in skipper's face appears on the big screen and there is nothing but sheer determination etched across it. And it shows with his penalty – a rocket of a shot straight down the middle of the goal.

Bayern Munich 3-2 Chelsea

Ivica Olic came on for Franck Ribery in extra-time for his final game for the club, but struggled to make an impact as he spurned a great chance to win it for his side from open play. He does the same in the shoot-out, side-footing the ball to Cech's left but at a comfortable height for him to palm it away with his 'wrong' hand.

Bayern Munich 3-2 Chelsea

One full-back has already converted from the spot in the shootout – can Ashley Cole make it two? The England international confidently slotted home his penalty four years ago in Moscow but this effort is even better as he sweeps his shot into the bottom left-hand corner and, as has been the case for almost the entire evening, the sides are inseparable once again.

Bayern Munich 3-3 Chelsea

Bastian Schweinsteiger was the hero for Bayern in their penalty shoot-out victory against Real Madrid in the semi-final and he is the man entrusted with taking the crucial fifth spot-kick here, too. He loses momentum with a stuttered run-up, though, and his low strike to the left-hand corner is too close to Cech, who superbly tips the ball onto the post. For the first time in this shoot-out he shows his true emotions with a double fist pump to the crowd. Chelsea now one spot-kick away from European glory!

Bayern Munich 3-3 Chelsea

Nine goals in nine cup finals, including the most dramatic of equalisers earlier in this game with Chelsea's dreams slipping away – it just has to be Didier Drogba stepping up with the chance to win it for the Blues. Neuer attempts mind games by jumping up and down on his line, hammering his palms against the crossbar as the Ivorian places the ball calmly and takes two steps back... and it's there! Drobga sends Neuer the wrong way and embraces Cech – eight years of heartache in the UEFA Champions League comes pouring out in jubilation as the Blues are crowned kings of Europe for the first time.

Bayern Munich 3-4 Chelsea

CHELSEA v BAYERN MUNICH: A STATISTICAL BREAKDOWN

Statistic	CHELSEA	FC BAYERN MÜNCHEN
Goals	1	1
Chance Conversion	17%	5%
Shots	6	21
Shooting Accuracy	50%	33%
Aerial Duels Won	65%	35%
Ground Duels Won	44%	54%
Recoveries	106	107
Saves Made	86%	67%
Pass Accuracy	83%	87%

TOP FIVE PLAYERS FOR PASS ACCURACY

Rank	Player name	Club	Accuracy
1	Gary Cahill	Chelsea	98%
2	Ashley Cole	Chelsea	95%
3	Philipp Lahm	Bayern Munich	93%
4	Salomon Kalou	Chelsea	92%
5	Diego Contento	Bayern Munich	92%

TOP FIVE PLAYERS FOR RECOVERIES

Rank	Player name	Club	Recoveries
1	John Mikel Obi	Chelsea	16
2	Philipp Lahm	Bayern Munich	16
3	José Bosingwa	Chelsea	11
4	Frank Lampard	Chelsea	11
5	Petr Cech	Chelsea	11

TOP FIVE PLAYERS FOR SUCCESSFUL DRIBBLES

Rank	Player name	Club	Dribbles
1	Fernando Torres	Chelsea	4
2	Franck Ribery	Bayern Munich	3
3	Salomon Kalou	Chelsea	2
4	Bastian Schweinsteiger	Bayern Munich	2
5	Ivica Olic	Bayern Munich	1

THE FINAL
RECKONING

Chelsea's final destination on their incredible
European journey was the Fussball Arena München,
where they lined up ready to make history . . .

Petr Cech:

"There were six penalties and I went the right way all the time and saved three, so I was well prepared. This is amazing, it's incredible, we finally got it. I said prior to the game that if we win the Cup, I don't want a cake (Cech's birthday was the day after the game), and this is the best present I can get. It's a dream come true."

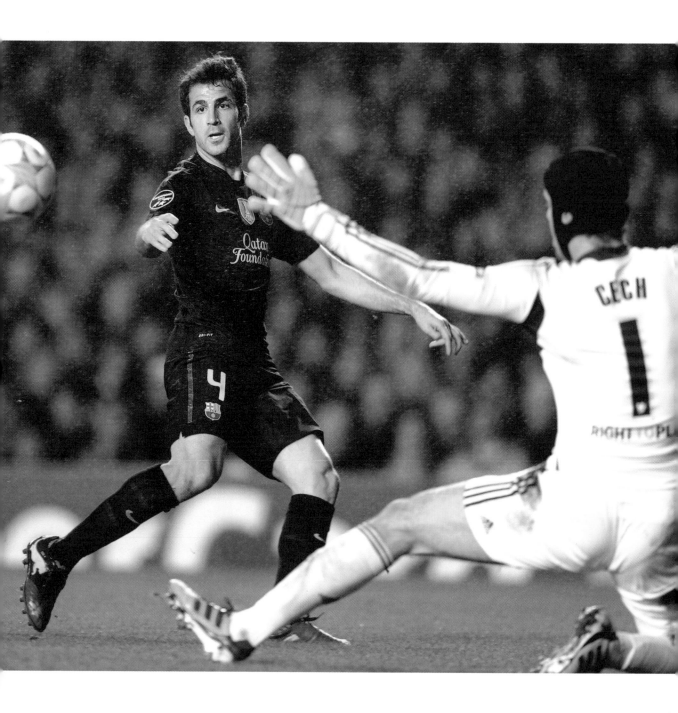

2011/12 UEFA
Champions League record:

Appearances: 13

Goals: 0

Petr the great

• The only player to appear in every game, Cech made no fewer than three penalty saves during the final, two in the shoot-out and one from Arjen Robben in extra-time.

• He was also brilliant during both legs of the semi-final, repeatedly repelling Barcelona's advances with a series of stupendous saves. Lionel Messi, Andres Iniesta, Javier Mascherano, Adriano and Carlos Puyol were among the players denied by the big Czech.

• Throughout the campaign he produced magnificent stops at crucial moments, notably from Oscar Cardoza against Benfica at the Bridge.

• Made several early saves in Naples, with Edinson Cavani and Christian Maggio denied.

• Kept out former Blue Michael Ballack against Bayer Leverkusen home and away.

185

Ashley Cole:

"You need luck in this competition and we rode our luck today but we deserved it.

   With the players we've got here, we knew we had time and with Petr making good saves like that, we always knew we were in it.

   I'm lost for words, we stuck to our tactics and in the end we deserved it. We looked up at the clock and realised we still had time left and we always believed. Now no-one can say anything to me. This is the reason I came here."

2011/12 UEFA Champions League record:

Appearances: 11 (+1 sub)

Goals: 0

World-class Cole

• It was another magnificent campaign for Cole, who married superb consistency with several crucial interventions at decisive moments.

• In the final, he largely nullified the threat posed by Arjen Robben and gave virtually a faultless performance. To top it off, he scored in the penalty shoot-out.

• Cleared off the line from Cesc Fabregas in Camp Nou against Barcelona.

• Perhaps no contribution was more important than when he cleared off the line from Christian Maggio in Naples when Chelsea were already trailing 3-1 in the first leg. A deficit of 4-1 may have been too much to come back from.

• Further forward, Cole earned a penalty against Benfica at Stamford Bridge which Frank Lampard converted.

189

David Luiz:

"It was an unbelievable night. I am so happy and emotional and my team-mates deserve this. We have worked so hard all this season and now to win this big cup is fantastic.

Roberto Di Matteo asked if I could help him and I said I will help you always, with one leg, two legs, or with no body. Roberto has been a fantastic coach and Andre Villas-Boas deserves it too as he has worked on this UEFA Champions League, and he is a fantastic coach as well. We have won two titles with Di Matteo and he deserves a great future.

There was always belief, and this team plays together. I have fantastic team-mates and there is a fantastic atmosphere every day in training. The people outside always try to kill Chelsea – saying Chelsea is not a good team, Chelsea don't have the players, Chelsea are old players, Chelsea don't have good young players – but now we showed the world who is Chelsea!"

2011/12 UEFA
Champions League record:

Appearances: 11

Goals: 1

The hair apparent

• Scored the first Chelsea goal of the UEFA Champions League campaign, firing in stylishly against Bayer Leverkusen in a match the Blues went on to win 2-0.

• Was the first Chelsea player to score in the penalty shoot-out in the final, and he did so with a flourish. If he had missed, it would have been a long way back from 2-0 down after two penalties each.

• Blocked an effort from Oscar Cardoza in the Estadio da Luz when the first leg between Benfica and Chelsea was 0-0.

Frank Lampard:

"I've never been so emotional in a game. Players were crying. Football can do that to people.

No one wants to have sad moments and miss out. You try to avoid the question when people ask if you think you will ever win it because you don't want to sound too desperate.

The UEFA Champions League gets harder every year because the other teams develop so much; Barcelona, Real Madrid, the Italian and German teams, they are better every season. So, I did kind of wonder if we'd ever win it.

But the circumstances of the season, to come from where we were to where we are now, make this feel absolutely massive. I have loved every league title and every FA Cup, but this one has become the one we all wanted. The owner wanted it, the club wanted it – and the club deserved it. On this night, we deserved it.

I have never seen a focus in a team like the one we travelled here with. You get a feeling your name is on the Cup. I'd have hated to say that beforehand because you look a fool when it doesn't happen. But we've had enough bad luck in this competition over the years. We've come to Bayern's home stadium and we've defended for our lives.

People threw their bodies in the way of the ball. Even in the penalties, when we normally think against Germans that it is game over, we managed to do it.

Roberto Di Matteo has to take a lot of credit. He brought a confidence and spirit to the group."

195

2011/12 UEFA
Champions League record:

Appearances: 8 (+ 4 subs)
Goals: 3

Frank's crowning glory

• What more can be said about Frank Lampard? He is the ultimate professional and the mainstay of our central midfield. His influence grew as the competition developed.

• It was Lampard's sublime pass that released Ramires for the oh-so-crucial goal in Camp Nou that resuscitated Chelsea's belief in first-half stoppage time, and provided a platform for the heroics of the second period.

• Frank also found Ramires with a cross-field pass in the first leg of the semi-final to set up the move that led to Didier Drogba's goal at Stamford Bridge.

197

• Scored at Valencia and converted penalties with trademark coolness in tense second legs with Napoli and Benfica, not to mention his unstoppable effort in the final shoot-out.

Fernando Torres:

"We needed to attack. We were playing like we had the handbrake on, looking like we couldn't attack, but I think we could, and in extra time we showed we could play counter-attack as well.

We had good luck at the right time, but I think we're the right team to win this. It's for these guys [the Chelsea fans]. They have been supporting us all season, a very difficult season when no one believed in us, a lot of ups and downs. At the end, they are the ones who deserve it."

2011/12 UEFA
Champions League record:

Appearances: 6 (+ 4 subs)
Goals: 3

Fantastic Fernando...

• The Spanish striker made several key contributions along the way, scoring three goals and creating chances for team-mates in an unselfish manner.

• It was Torres who won the corner from which Didier Drogba equalised three minutes from time in the UEFA Champions League Final.

• There was the unforgettable moment when he ran clear at Camp Nou, evaded Victor Valdes and stroked the ball into the empty net to confirm the club's participation in the UEFA Champions League Final.

• Scored twice in the 5-0 demolition of Genk and only heroic goalkeeping and defending prevented him from adding to his tally.

• Provided assists for Ramires against Genk away, Juan Mata at home to Bayer Leverkusen and Salomon Kalou against Benfica.

201

Juan Mata:

"It's a dream come true. It's my first year here at Chelsea and we have won the most important trophy in the final of the UEFA Champions League so we are very, very happy.

I think the most important moment in the game was the goal of Didier. We were losing with almost 90 minutes on the clock and we got back in the game.

During extra-time we ran a lot and we defended well. Penalties are a lottery and it was amazing for us."

2011/12 UEFA
Champions League record:

Appearances: 11 (+ 1 sub)
Goals: 1

He's the Juan

• Juan Mata's first season with Chelsea saw the talented Spaniard demonstrate consistent excellence and contribute hugely to the Blues' triumphs.

• He was on target in the first game of the campaign to seal a 2-0 victory over Bayer Leverkusen at Stamford Bridge.

• Provided a composed finish to give the Blues the lead in Naples. Although we went on to lose the game 3-1, Mata's goal kept us in touch for the second leg and provided a platform for a magnificent comeback.

• Slipped the ball through for Didier Drogba to seal a 3-0 victory over Valencia in the final group game, which ensured qualification for the knockout stage.

205

Didier Drogba:

"This is my happiest moment in football, big time. I don't have enough words to describe this moment and I am just happy for the team and the fans.

When Bayern scored, I was really disappointed. I was thinking, 'No, not again.' The good thing is Juan Mata just came and said, 'We have to believe.' And, a few seconds after, we scored from his corner. So, it is like a dream and really I am happy.

We deserve it and we make very good champions because we beat the ex-champions of Europe, Barcelona, and we had to come out of a difficult situation with Napoli and playing Benfica wasn't easy at all. Also, beating Bayern Munich at their stadium with all these fans in red, I think we deserve to be champions. I think this win defines this whole European campaign. It's really extraordinary what happened to us. It was our moment to win.

We believed it against Napoli, because we lost 3-1 [in the first leg] and in the last minute Ashley Cole cleared one off the line to spare us a 4-1 loss and allowed us to believe. Many didn't believe in us, but we did and that is why we went to the very end."

207

2011/12 UEFA Champions League record:

Appearances: 7 (+ 1 sub)

Goals: 6

Signing off in style

• What a way to say goodbye. In many ways, Didier Drogba, a force of nature all by himself, propelled Chelsea throughout the glorious campaign.

• Of course, when we reflect on his contributions, what immediately comes to mind are the trophy-clinching penalty and thunderous header that kept the Blues alive, three minutes before the end of the final.

• He scored the only goal in the semi-final first leg victory over Barcelona at Stamford Bridge, which gave us a crucial advantage for the trip to Camp Nou.

• Was on the mark twice in the win over Valencia in the final group game that ensured progression to the knockout phase.

• Sparked the comeback against Napoli with the first goal. Also provided the cross for Branislav Ivanovic to complete the night's work.

209

John Mikel Obi:

"The owner has made it clear to us that this trophy is the one he wants to win. And now that we have done that, I think that he is a very, very happy man. We have shown what we can do. And, hopefully, people can stop writing us off.

I think we have made names for ourselves - we are the first club to win this trophy from London. I think it is just fantastic, it is amazing."

2011/12 UEFA Champions League record:

Appearances: 7 (+ 2 subs)
Goals: 0

Our enforcer

• As ever, John Mikel Obi provided a reassuring and dynamic presence at the base of our midfield throughout the campaign.

• His contribution and concentration was vital during the 180 minutes of action against Barcelona, much of it spent under siege. Mikel shielded the backline from the Catalan's array of talent, most notably Lionel Messi, and did so much to protect our hard-won advantage.

• In the final he helped largely nullify the threat of Arjen Robben and Franck Ribery as they cut in from the flanks.

213

Florent Malouda:

"It was a match between two quality teams. I lost the World Cup on penalties in 2006 and then the UEFA Champions League final in 2008, which makes this victory even more special. Now we have to enjoy this with our families and the Chelsea supporters."

2011/12 UEFA Champions League record:

Appearances: 5 (+ 4 subs)

Goals: 0

Florent happy to assist

• Florent Malouda made several key contributions, often from the substitute's bench. Early in the campaign he picked out Frank Lampard in the box for a crucial goal in the 1-1 draw with Valencia in the Mestalla and was influential in the following game, setting the attacking tone in the 5-0 win over Genk at Stamford Bridge.

• Despite suffering a hamstring injury in the final Premier League game of the season, Malouda was able to come on in the final, replacing Ryan Bertrand in the 72nd minute. His pace and unpredictability gave Bayern plenty to think about.

217

2011/12 UEFA
Champions League record:

Appearances: 7 (+ 4 subs)
Goals: 0

Jose at the double

• Bosingwa signed off his Chelsea career in style. He played the entire 120 minutes of the final, carrying out with aplomb the task of keeping Franck Ribery quiet down the right wing.

• The Portuguese defender came on after only 12 minutes in the UEFA Champions League semi-final, second leg, against Barcelona at Camp Nou to replace an injured Gary Cahill.

• The UEFA Champions League triumph was the second time that Bosingwa had tasted glory in Europe's biggest club competition on German soil. He also lifted the trophy in 2004, having been on the bench when Porto defeated Monaco in the showpiece at Arena AufSchalke, Gelsenkirchen.

219

Salomon Kalou:

"It was destiny for us to win it. It was also team spirit and togetherness. Put it together and it's a wonderful moment for us to win the cup."

2011/12 UEFA Champions League record:

Appearances: 3 (+4 sub)

Goals: 2

Salomon's final flourish

• Kalou scored in our 5-0 rout of Genk at Stamford Bridge during the group stages and notched the only goal of the game in the first leg of the quarter-final, away to Benfica.

• The Ivory Coast international almost broke the deadlock in the UEFA Champions League Final shortly before half-time. Dider Drogba and Frank Lampard combined to find him on the right, only for Manuel Neuer to save the low-drilled effort.

• The UEFA Champions League Final saw Kalou leave the Blues on a high note, as he moved to Ligue 1 side Lille on a four-year deal in the close season.

223

Gary Cahill:

"When I picked up the injury against Barcelona I feared I wouldn't make the game, but I am thankful to the staff that got David [Luiz] and me back.

It's absolutely amazing. The team has stuck together throughout everything and we've won two trophies.

People thought we were dead and buried against Napoli, against Barcelona, but we kept coming back. Bayern played some fantastic football, they had a lot of corners, but we defended well and it's all paid off.

I made the move to win trophies. I signed for five-and-a-half years and have won two in six months. If you told me at the start of the season I would win the UEFA Champions League I would have thought you were joking. It's unbelievable."

225

2011/12 UEFA Champions League record:

Appearances: 4 (+ 1 sub)

Goals: 0

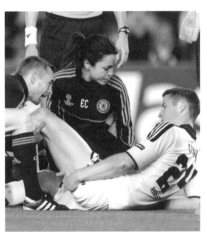

Cahill's perfect start

• He only arrived at the club in January 2012 but Gary Cahill was hugely important to Chelsea's UEFA Champions League success.

• Cahill performed brilliantly in the final, sharing central defensive duties with David Luiz following John Terry's suspension. His participation had been in doubt after he picked up a hamstring injury in the early stages of the semi-final second leg in Barcelona.

• The 26-year-old was excellent in the first leg of the semi-final, helping keep Barca at bay and ensuring we held a 1-0 lead for part two.

227

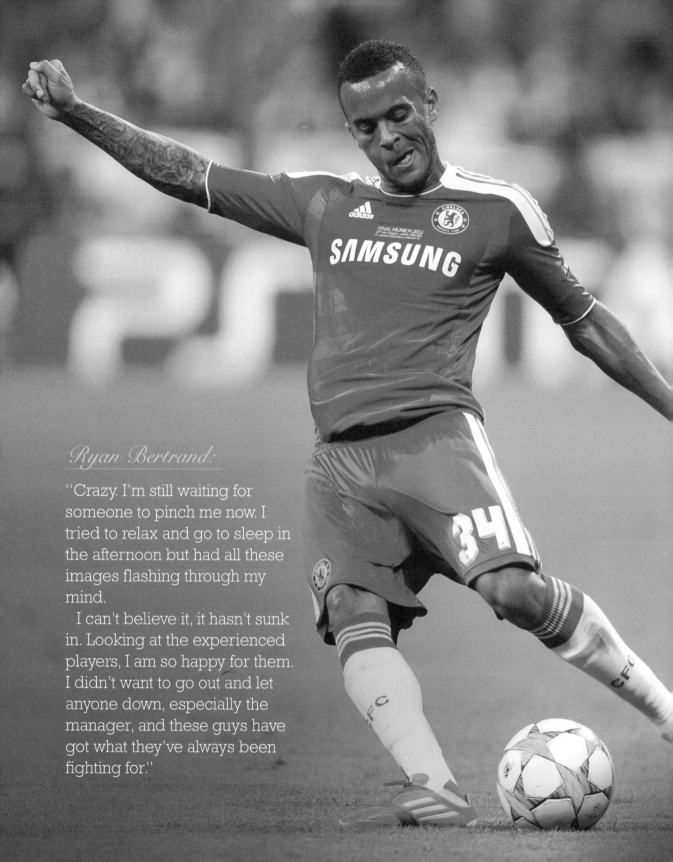

Ryan Bertrand:

''Crazy. I'm still waiting for someone to pinch me now. I tried to relax and go to sleep in the afternoon but had all these images flashing through my mind.

I can't believe it, it hasn't sunk in. Looking at the experienced players, I am so happy for them. I didn't want to go out and let anyone down, especially the manager, and these guys have got what they've always been fighting for.''

2011/12 UEFA Champions League record:

Appearances: 1

Goals: 0

A final call for Ryan

• There is no bigger introduction to UEFA Champions League football than making your debut in the competition in the final – but that is exactly what happened to Ryan Bertrand.

• Despite being only 22 years old at the time, and playing outside of his favoured left-back position, Bertrand showed composure on the left flank of the midfield.

• Bertrand's defensive expertise was used in a more forward position to keep Bayern Munich's wingers and right back Philipp Lahm at bay.

• The final was only Bertrand's 13th start for the Blues and he executed his role to a tee before being replaced by Florent Malouda with less than 20 minutes of normal time to play.

229

Branislav Ivanovic, Ramires, Raul Meireles, John Terry…

Their contribution to Chelsea's successful UEFA Champions League campaign will not be forgotten.

John Terry, Branislav Ivanovic, Ramires and Raul Meireles were unavailable for selection in Munich because of suspensions accrued in the second leg of the semi-final against Barcelona.

It was a bittersweet European season for the Chelsea skipper, who lifted the UEFA Champions League trophy with Frank Lampard. During the campaign JT was his usual inspirational self at the heart of defence, marshalling everyone around him and offering maximum protection to the Blues' goal.

He scored a trademark header from a Lampard corner to give us the advantage in the second leg against Napoli. Terry was also magnificent in the first leg against Barcelona at the Bridge to shut out one of the most dazzling attacking teams of all time.

Ivanovic also had an excellent European campaign for the Blues, making significant contributions in defence and attack. He was on target in the 5-0 group stage defeat of Genk at Stamford Bridge, heading in a Florent Malouda free-kick for the Blues' fourth goal of the evening.

Most notably, of course, he completed the comeback against Napoli on a raucous night in the first knockout round. After a 3-1 defeat in Naples, the Blues were leading 3-1 at home in a match that had moved into a tense half-hour of extra-time.

With the first period drawing to a conclusion, Didier Drogba managed to find

231

some space on the right wing and crossed low for Ivanovic who absolutely thumped the ball into the net from 10 yards.

A primeval roar rang out around Stamford Bridge for a goal that took the Blues into the quarter-finals.

Ramires electrified Chelsea's play throughout the run to Munich. His awareness and acceleration unsettled opposition defences and often left them floundering. His exquisite chip in first-half stoppage time in Camp Nou changed the whole momentum of the match after 45 minutes when the Blues had conceded two and seen their captain sent off. If that goal had not arrived when it did, Chelsea's task in the second half may have been insurmountable.

He was also on target in Genk having linked up well with Fernando Torres and scored the second goal in the 3-0 defeat of Valencia.

The Brazilian was often a creator as well as the finisher. He crossed for Didier Drogba to give us a crucial lead in the first leg of the semi-final. He also set up Drogba's first goal in the second leg with Napoli.

For Raul Meireles, his decision to move to London from Liverpool in August was richly rewarded as the FA Cup and UEFA Champions League were won. Unfortunately he wasn't able to play in the Munich final but he did much to ensure Chelsea got there.

The quarter-final second leg against Benfica was ending in high tension with the Blues ahead 2-1 on aggregate but one opposition strike away from going out on the away goals rule. The Portuguese midfielder banished the anxiety with a run from his own half which he concluded with a powerful shot that flew into the net. Tie over and into the semi-finals we went.

Meireles was also on target with a shot from distance in the comprehensive victory over Genk, opening the scoring and later providing the cross for Torres to head the third goal.

Roberto Di Matteo:

"Football and life are unpredictable at times and crazy. I don't think we could have predicted what's happened over the last three months at the club; it's been very difficult, but to finish like this is an incredible achievement.

It feels great. You think about it when you watch at home, watching others lift the trophy, but I'm pleased for the players. They've worked so hard over the years to win it.

When Bayern Munich scored there wasn't much time left, but the heart and passion we've shown in the competition has been immense.

To be able to equalise and go into extra time was a good feeling. Preparation for the game was difficult with suspensions and injuries. It wasn't ideal for a UEFA Champions League Final, but the desire and motivation has shown again. I'm very happy to make history. It's the first time we've won it – the UEFA Champions League is very difficult to win and you have to take your chances when they come.

It was a great team effort. We always tend to focus on the goalscorers, but Petr Cech saved a penalty, while Ashley Cole saved off the line in Napoli, which gave us hope for the second leg.

Penalties are a lottery, but Bayern were very good. They played well and are a good team – that's why they've won it many times before – but our supporters will be delighted because we've won the UEFA Champions League."

235

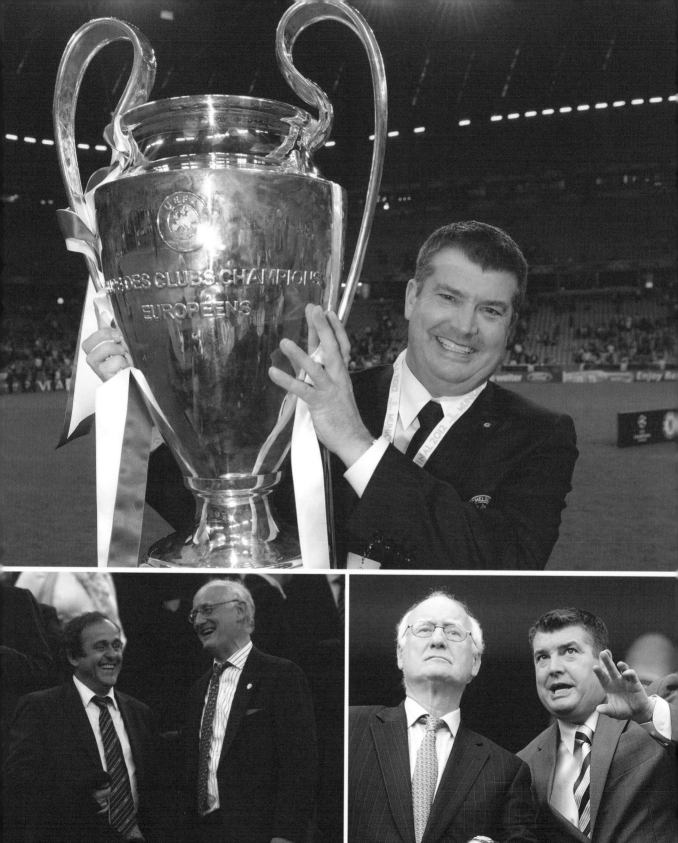

Bruce Buck:

"Roman gave a thank-you speech and the message was that it was all down to the boys.

As for our ambition, there are a lot of teams with three or four of those stars [on their shirts] out there. We have one.

Robbie has done an amazing job and he's enabled these players to get back the confidence that they used to have and which they need to perform. He's really got the players performing and we're very proud of him."

Ron Gourlay:

"We did it and it feels absolutely fantastic. It has been a real up and down season, with a lot of pressure on a lot of people and this is really special. It's an incredible story.

This is the only piece of silverware that's been missing for us. We've had a great time domestically since the owner came on board, and this just adds to that and allows us to take things to the next level. This is the elite trophy in Europe and it's phenomenal for everybody at the club, especially the fans who were fantastic on the night. Even when we went 1-0 down, they stayed with us and pushed the team on because they believed we could do it.

Let's not forget we had four players missing, two centre halves who hadn't played for nearly a month, a young player out of position in Ryan Bertrand and we had to take penalties at the Bayern end, so there were quite a few obstacles to overcome. They're big, big players and we've seen them perform in cup finals and crucial games before and they've done it once again. We're all very proud of them."

237

Pat Nevin:

"The current golden generation has been together for quite a few years now, so – for Didier, Frank, JT, Petr and Ashley in particular – it must have felt like an eternity hoping this day would come, and maybe even secretly thinking that it might never happen.

The thing is, it is even longer than that – you have to go all the way through the club's proud history and the great players that have played here to fully understand how long this journey has been. Every player who has played for the club feels the same way; it isn't a case of "I wish it was me" but, quite simply, "Our club finally got there."

Ron Harris:

"Having gone so close to winning it four years ago, when it came down to penalties again my first thought was, "I hope it doesn't happen again!" However, the lads did brilliantly and it's a fantastic achievement by everyone at the club.

It looked like Chelsea had lost the game on a few occasions, but I'm a great believer that if your name's on the trophy, your name is on the trophy!

We need to give the lads some credit for the way they got back into it and then the composure they showed from the penalty spot, especially after Juan Mata missed the first. I was definitely very confident when Drogba stepped up."

239

Gianfranco Zola:

"For Chelsea, the [UEFA Champions League] final in Munich was extraordinary. The atmosphere was unforgettable."

Ruud Gullit:

"We had a memorable evening, all the more so because this was an achievement that seemed to be written in the stars. Ever since they had overturned the 3-1 deficit to Napoli, I believed the UEFA Champions League held Chelsea's destiny. Against Bayern Munich, they did not bring their most beautiful football but, defensively, they did what was necessary.

I embraced Didier Drogba on the pitch [after the final], full of pride at the display he had delivered. For a lifetime Chelsea fans will recall his final penalty, but I was struck more by his brilliant technique for the header that brought Chelsea back from the brink.

And if this truly is the end of the career, he will always have the comfort of knowing that his final kick brought Chelsea the greatest prize in club football. Chelsea are firmly among the big boys of Europe now and, more significantly, a part of history. I could not be more proud."

Gus Poyet:

"You can call my feelings "double happiness" – I am feeling this way not only because of Chelsea, but also because it was Robbie. That made it so, so special for me and my family. Absolutely incredible.

When I saw his face after the final it made me so happy – and I hope that he believed me when I kept saying to him beforehand that they were going to win it!

I wasn't just saying it because I wanted to be nice, I had this feeling that Chelsea were going to win the final. I call Robbie "one of us" as he is one of the Chelsea boys and I'm so happy to see him and the club enjoy this moment."

241

TRUE BLUE TRIUMPH

Although Bayern may have been very much at home, Chelsea's fans helped paint Munich blue as they descended on the German city en masse to inspire their team to an unforgettable triumph.

Along the sun-drenched streets of the nation's football capital, supporters of both clubs mixed in good spirits, singing their hearts out, eating, drinking and engaging in good-natured, friendly banter.

The Odeonsplatz, a square in central Munich, was allocated to Blues' followers who created a fantastic festival-like atmosphere in the build-up to the match.

Across town at the Olympiapark, which hosted the 1972 Olympic Games and was the former home of Bayern, both sets of supporters mingled freely while enjoying the sights and sounds of what UEFA had on offer, trying their hand at various skills tests, watching classic games and visiting the UEFA Champions League museum, or simply soaking up the sun.

The main event was in the old Olympic Stadium, also scene of the 1974 World Cup Final, where a match billed as World All-Stars v Bayern All-Stars and Friends ended in a 3-2 victory for the World side containing several Chelsea players.

Coached by Ruud Gullit, there were spells on the pitch for Gianfranco Zola, Graeme Le Saux and Celestine Babayaro among a line-up that could point to a serious number of winners' medals in major competitions.

243

Throughout the day the Blues' fans gave their heroes magnificent backing, singing their hearts out once inside the stadium and roaring them on to ultimate glory.

CHAMPIO
OF EUROPE

HOMECOMING KINGS

The Chelsea boys returned home as conquering heroes with two glittering prizes to show off, and the fans came out in force to scream their approval.

It was the first time in the 57-year history of the European Cup that it had been paraded through the streets of London as thousands of fans lined the streets of Fulham as an open-top bus made its way from Stamford Bridge to Parson's Green.

And we must not forget that the FA Cup was also along for the ride, as it was for the 2010 Double winning parade, only that time it shared the bus with the Premier League Trophy.

The parade set off from the stadium's west entrance before travelling east along Fulham Road.

It turned right into Hortensia Road and then right again on to King's Road, before going down New King's Road.

The blue-clad, flag-waving, celery-throwing, whistle and horn-blowing throng had been growing for hours and matched that of 1997 when a long wait for silverware ended with an FA Cup victory, and that of 2005 when an even longer wait for a league win came to an end. Every vantage point was filled.

The players and staff arrived at the Bridge from Heathrow Airport shortly before the 4pm parade start

(continues on p253) ▶

249

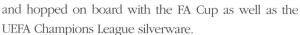

and hopped on board with the FA Cup as well as the UEFA Champions League silverware.

As with other recent parades the largest gathering was at Eel Brook Common where a big screen was located and Chelsea TV were broadcasting live. There the bus stopped for some communal singing with the European-flavoured 'Champione, champione, ole, ole, ole' a popular choice, frequently led by captain John Terry.

David Luiz led the crowd through a more traditional 'Blue is the Colour', Gary Cahill announced he was going to bounce in a minute and 'Happy Birthday' was sung to penalty shoot-out hero Petr Cech who turned 30 on the day.

Didier Drogba was prominent in the parade and received plenty of cheers. Frank Lampard took the microphone to say that the Saturday night had been the best of the players' careers and that Chelsea was the best club in the world, before John Terry told the fans how much they deserved to win the UEFA Champions League.

253

2011/12
UEFA CHAMPIONS LEAGUE RESULTS

Date	Venue	Opponent	Score
Sep 13	H	Bayer Leverkusen (Group E)	W 2-0
Sep 28	A	Valencia (Group E)	D 1-1
Oct 19	H	KRC Genk (Group E)	W 5-0
Nov 1	A	KRC Genk (Group E)	D 1-1
Nov 23	A	Bayer Leverkusen (Group E)	L 1-2
Dec 6	H	Valencia (Group E)	W 3-0
Feb 21	A	Napoli (Round of 16)	L 1-3
Mar 14	H	Napoli (Round of 16)	W 4-1 aet
Mar 27	A	Benfica (Quarter-final)	W 1-0
Apr 4	H	Benfica (Quarter-final)	W 2-1
Apr 18	H	Barcelona (Semi-final)	W 1-0
Apr 24	A	Barcelona (Semi-final)	D 2-2
May 19	N	Bayern Munich (Final) Won 4-3 on penalties	D 1-1 aet

Appearances (13): **Cech 13, Cole 11(1), Mata 11(1), D Luiz 11, Ivanovic 10, Ramires 10, Meireles 9(2), Lampard 8(4), Terry 8, Bosingwa 7(4), Mikel 7(2), Drogba 7(1), Torres 6(4), Malouda 5(4), Sturridge 5(2), Cahill 4(1), Kalou 3(4), Romeu 3, Anelka 2(2), Essien 1(1), Ferreira 1(1), Bertrand 1, Alex 0(3).** *Substitute appearances in brackets*

Goals (25): **Drogba 6, Lampard 3, Ramires 3, Torres 3, Ivanovic 2, Kalou 2, Mata 2, Meireles 2, D Luiz 1, Terry 1.**

Goals Against (12): **Lavezzi (Napoli) 2, Busquets (Barcelona) 1, Cavani (Napoli) 1, Derdiyok (Bayer Leverkusen) 1, Friedrich (Bayer Leverkusen) 1, Garcia (Benfica) 1, Iniesta (Barcelona) 1, Inler (Napoli) 1, Muller (Bayern Munich) 1, Soldado (Valencia) 1, Vossen (KRC Genk) 1.**

Minutes On Pitch (1,289): **Cech 1,289, Cole 1,138, D Luiz 1,056, Mata 983, Ivanovic 973, Lampard 891, Ramires 888, Meireles 795, Mikel 738, Bosingwa 720, Drogba 700, Torres 671, Terry 669, Malouda 564, Sturridge 450, Cahill 365, Kalou 354, Romeu 262, Anelka 209, Essien 149, Ferreira 126, Bertrand 74, Alex 56.**

Penalties Awarded (6): ***Chelsea (3):* D Luiz 1 (KRC Genk a, saved), Lampard 2 (Napoli h, Benfica h). *Opponents (3):* Soldado 1 (Valencia a), Messi 1 (Barcelona a, missed), Robben 1 (Bayern Munich, saved Cech).**

Strikes On Woodwork (11): ***Chelsea (4):* Mata 1, Meireles 1, Sturridge 1, Torres 1. *Opponents (7):* Ballack (Bayer Leverkusen), Alba (Valencia), Sanchez (Barcelona), Pedro Rodriguez (Barcelona), Messi 2 (Barcelona), Robben (Bayern Munich).**

Top **All-Time** UEFA Champions League Appearances (excludes qualifying games): **Terry 85, Lampard 81(7), Cech 75, Drogba 60(9), A Cole 49(1), Makelele 47(2), Carvalho 46(1), Essien 45(4), J Cole 36(15), Malouda 36(11), Mikel 32(9), Ballack 31(2), Gallas 30, Ivanovic 30, Ferreira 26(7), Kalou 24(25).** *Substitute appearances in brackets*

Top **All-Time** UEFA Champions League Scorers (excludes qualifying games): **Drogba 34, Lampard 22 (3 pens), Anelka 12 (1 pen), Flo 8, Terry 8, Kalou 7, J Cole 6, Essien 6, Ivanovic 6, Ballack 4 (1 pen), Crespo 4, Gudjohnsen 4, Shevchenko 4, Wise 4.**

English Winners Of The European Cup/UEFA Champions League (12): **Liverpool 5, Manchester United 3, Nottingham Forest 2, Chelsea 1, Aston Villa 1.**

255